Contents

Bookkeeping Basics
for
Freelance Writers

By Brigitte A. Thompson

Crystal Press
Simi Valley, California

Published by Crystal Press
Edited by Chelsea Baxter

ISBN-13: 978-0-9632123-8-2
ISBN-10: 0-9632123-8-9

10 9 8 7 6 5 4 3 2

Crystal Press
1750 Orr Avenue
Simi Valley, CA 93065
805-527-4369

Printed in the United States of America

Introduction

Congratulations! You, along with thousands of other writers, have started your own business.

Your computer is plugged in, shelves are stocked with supplies, and you have freelance work lined up. You feel ready to get started, but has anything been overlooked?

If you are like the majority of new business owners, recordkeeping is the last thing on your mind at this point. With all the excitement surrounding this new adventure, it is hard to think about seemingly trivial matters such as how income should be recorded and what expenses should be tracked. However, bookkeeping is essential and can help reduce your taxes, which can save you money.

Bookkeeping Basics for Freelance Writers addresses issues writers face daily such as how to deduct travel expenses, determine your taxable writing income, and claim home office deductions. This book will also help you become organized and understand how to hold onto every dollar you are legally allowed to keep.

Navigating through the recordkeeping required for a small business owner can be difficult. This book is written exclusively for those of us who earn money by writing. It will include useful information to help you interpret the complexities of our federal tax code and proven techniques to reduce your taxable income.

In order to provide something tangible to follow, you will be able to view the recordkeeping forms for a fictitious writing business, Write Now. The completed forms will allow you to visualize each step in this recordkeeping system.

You can use these same forms to fill in your own information for your business. These examples will provide the information you need to complete your business federal tax return. They are designed to be quick and easy to fill out.

The few minutes it takes to complete the forms can reduce your taxable income and help you save money. If you prefer to hire a tax preparer, you can use this organized system and benefit by capturing all the business deductions you are allowed to claim. By understanding the recordkeeping required to operate your business, you will be well on your way to financial success!

Most states require that you become registered with them in order to operate a business. Before you start, you will need to investigate local, state, and federal regulations to determine which apply to your business. Be sure to take the time to find out the rules and follow them.

Throughout the book we have included tips from both new and seasoned writers. In the Tips for Success feature (as shown to the left) writers share the wisdom they have acquired over time. In the Writer's Block feature (as shown below) you will discover specific questions writers have submitted to me which, when answered, help clarify points made about that topic.

You will also find that each part of this book works together to assist you in forming your overall business plan. Each chapter steps through a comprehensive plan that works as a building block towards a successful writing business.

My goal with this book is to help you become an expert in the recordkeeping required to operate a writing business. You may write for a newspaper, provide copy for Web sites, freelance for magazines, or be working on a manuscript. This book applies to all of us who put thoughts and research onto paper.

By understanding and utilizing the information explained in this book, you should be able to reduce your taxable income, pay the least amount of taxes, and obtain a completely organized business recordkeeping system.

This book will help you build the foundation for success.

Writer's Block

My writing business consists of just me, myself, and I. I'm an employed reporter by day and freelance movie critic by night. I write movie reviews for our local newspaper. If time is tight and the deadline is looming, I sometimes hire a local college student to do my typing. Do I really have to go through all the work involved to get her to complete a Subcontractor Agreement?
—Nick in Florida

Yes, you can skip ahead to Chapter 7 to learn more about the difference between an employee and a subcontractor, but this college student will be classified as one or the other. If she's determined to be an employee, there are a whole bunch of taxes you are going to have to learn how to track and submit to both state and federal agencies. If she's determined to be a subcontractor, itís less paperwork, but still the responsibility falls to you as the business owner paying her. Unfortunately, having the appropriate paperwork completed is a requirement. On the plus side, paying for the typing generates a nice, completely deductible, business expense which will lower your taxable income.

Chapter 1

Getting Started

Before you start your own business, there are several decisions you will need to consider. Some of these decisions will affect how you file your taxes, such as which form of legal organization you choose when starting your business. It is also important to be organized and have an understanding of basic bookkeeping and accounting methods. This will help you easily see the taxable portion of your income and any business expenses that can be deducted. The forms in this chapter will help you understand how the decisions you make regarding your business will influence how you file your taxes.

Legal Organization

There are several forms of legal organization to choose from when establishing your business. The most common form for a writer is a sole proprietorship, but you should understand the choices and speak to a lawyer, accountant, or tax preparer to find out which option is the best for you.

This decision will influence the taxes you pay, the extent of your liability, and the way business transactions are reported to the Internal Revenue Service (IRS).

Sole Proprietorship

The easiest business to set up is the sole proprietorship. This is described by Publication 583 *Starting a Business and Keeping Records* of the Internal Revenue Service as the simplest form of business organization and is the default classification for a business owned by one person. The IRS does not require fees or special forms to set up this business. You can conduct business under your name or create a business name. If you choose to use a name other than your own, be sure to register it with the appropriate state department. As a sole proprietor, you are the business and all personal as well as business assets are at risk. Despite how easy it is to be a sole proprietor, this *unlimited liability* is worth careful consideration.

S-Corporation

Establishing your business as an S-Corporation will provide you with *limited liability* that will create a clear line between you and your business. There are forms to be filed and fees to be paid in most states in order to obtain this status. Your business will need a name which must be registered with your Secretary of State before doing business.

Since the business owner is considered to be separate from the business itself, some additional tax forms will need to be filed to report your earnings. An S-Corporation will file Federal Form 1120S annually from which a Schedule K-1 is generated. It is important to note that the S-Corporation itself does not pay income taxes therefore double taxation is not an issue.

The information on the K-1 will become incorporated into your personal 1040 tax return and the 1120S gets mailed separately. Undistributed profits under this organization are subject to applicable federal and state taxes, but are exempt from self-employment tax which is a wonderful benefit. When you opt to incorporate your business into an S-Corporation, you are no longer subject to self-employment taxes because you are no longer self-employed. As an S-Corporation, your business is a corporate entity entirely separate from you. You would issue yourself a paycheck as an employee of the corporation. The funds left over as net profit would be distributed to you and subject to fewer taxes than if you were self-employed. The IRS does scrutinize this area to ensure that wages paid to the owner of an S-Corporation are meeting the standards of "reasonable compensation" for each industry. This will be discussed more in depth in Chapter 9.

Partnership

If more than one person owns the business, it cannot be a sole proprietorship and a partnership may be worth considering. Similar to sole proprietorships, partnerships are easy to organize and maintain. A written agreement should be created between all partners called the Articles of Partnership that outlines the commencement date of the partnership, salaries, division of duties, and procedures for settling disputes. It is important to note that in a partnership, all parties are equally liable. This means you are legally connected to your partner(s) and their actions and/or inactions are your responsibility.

A partnership files a Form 1065 with the IRS every year and K-1 forms are issued to the partners. As with the S-Corporation, the partnership does not pay any income tax. Partnerships and S-Corporations are what is called "pass through entities." They do file tax returns, but no money is due for income taxes to the IRS from filing these returns.

Writer's Block

Do I need to get an EIN if I'm only a sole proprietor?
—Karla in New Mexico

In most circumstances you can file your writing business tax return as a sole proprietor using your Social Security number, but there are instances where you will need to obtain an EIN such as if you have an employee. The IRS offers a handy questionnaire which takes you through the process of making this decision. Type "Do I need an EIN" in the search field of their Web site and take the quiz to find out.

If you choose to establish your business as a partnership or S-Corporation, a separate identification number will be needed for IRS use. Form SS-4 is an Application for an Employer Identification Number (EIN) and it can be ordered through the IRS Web site. In addition, each state has its own requirements surrounding business legal status. Be sure to check in with local, city, and state departments to determine what forms must be filed based on your entity choice.

Which Business Form is Right for Me?

You may want to use this table to write down your thoughts on each form of business organization and list some questions that come to mind.

Legal Organization	Pros	Cons	Questions
Sole Proprietorship			
S-Corporation			
Partnership			
Other Options			

Choosing Your Business Name

What are you going to call your new business? You may use your own name in title such as *Brigitte's Writing Service* or create something clever such as *Write Now*. As mentioned earlier, if you will be using a business name that is not your own name, you must register the name with the Secretary of State's office in your own state and ensure the name is not already in use. There is normally a fee associated with this registration which varies by state.

The Secretary of State's office, however, does not determine whether the chosen name may infringe upon federally registered or common law trademarks. If you anticipate your writing business will build a national identity, then you may want to consider performing trademark searches before committing to a name. It may be cheaper to analyze the trademark issues up front than to take a chance with a legal dispute over the name later.

You can learn more about using a Federal Trade Name Registration by visiting the U.S. Small Business Administration's Web site.

Although a business name is not required, it can help create a professional image. You may want to consider the types of services you will be providing and name your business accordingly. Will you be writing primarily business or health articles for magazines? Will you concentrate on writing college textbooks or maybe provide editing and rewriting services for local universities? You want to be sure that when people see your business name, they understand what services you offer.

Consider the following business name examples and what comes into your mind when you read them.

> *Wonderful Moments, September Morning, Milton Express,*
> *Willard's World, Snowcap Enterprises*

From the name, can you tell what these businesses offer? No. The name you select for your writing business should tell the world what you do and leave no doubt as to what services are offered. Now consider the following business names.

> *Quality Editing Services, Ghostwriting for Celebrities, Comedic*
> *Copywriting, Inc., Index Express*

The names clearly speak for themselves.

Another very important part of your business name is its availability on the Internet as a dot com address. There are a variety of Web sites on the Internet who host domain names where you can type in the business name you have in mind to see if it is already in use. Although there are other site address options such as dot net or dot biz, the dot coms are still the most popular. Try your name at GoDaddy.com, NetworkSolutions.com or MyDomain.com.

Use the space provided to describe what services you wish to offer. The results may assist you in determining your business name.

Services I Will Offer

1. _____

2. _____

3. _____

4. _____

5. _____

6. _____

Possible Business Names

1. _____

2. _____

3. _____

4. _____

5. _____

6. _____

Bookkeeping Basics

It is important to establish a system of recordkeeping that works for you. Some things need to be recorded daily, while others can be done weekly or monthly. It is imperative that you get into the habit of saving and recording everything related to your business. All money you receive from your business must be recorded as income. You will be able to reduce the taxable portion of this income by deductible business expenses.

Tips for Success

"Becoming organized has been the single best thing I have done for my freelance career. To keep track of finances, know which visual method works best for you. I have writer friends that swear by their software programs while others prefer old fashioned paper ledgers."

Victoria Witchey
www.
VictoriaWitchey.com

Be Organized

Organization is necessary to operate any business. The forms enclosed in this book need to be maintained, and detailed information needs to be attached to each one of them to completely justify the expense. Once each form is completed, it needs to be filed or stored in a safe place until the time comes to prepare your income taxes. Some people find it helpful to create a simple filing system using folders and lined paper. Transactions can be recorded on sheets of 8 ½" by 11" paper attached to the front of each folder with supporting documentation filed inside. Folders can be labeled by category including one for recording income and another for expenses.

This information can be kept manually by handwritten record or you can transfer the data into a computer spreadsheet. Microsoft Excel® provides an easy to use program which can help you organize your records. The computerized ability to do mathematical equations can help reduce errors in compiling the numbers. If you would like to go a step further, Intuit® offers some user friendly accounting programs such as QuickBooks® which can generate financial statements and budgets using the data you record. Any system that works for you is acceptable, as long as the pertinent information is retained. Maintaining good records can help you manage your cash flow wisely and prepare you in the event of an audit.

Start a Separate Business Account

It is a good idea to obtain a separate checking account to be used for your writing business. The IRS requires business owners to differentiate between business and personal income and expenses. Although they do not require businesses to maintain a separate checking account, they do require a clear paper trail. Utilizing one bank account for personal transactions and another for business transactions makes it easier for you to create this documented trail. All of the money you receive from writing income should be deposited into this account and all of your business expenses should be written from this account.

Save Your Receipts

Without the receipt, you do not have a justifiable business deduction. Save every electric bill, save every invoice from your subscriptions, and save every receipt from supply purchases. If you do not have a receipt, you will need a cancelled check or credit card statement showing the charge. Even when banks do not return checks, they will store an image of the check for up to a year or they will include an image of your check with your monthly statement. Keep this information as it will help prove the expense in the event of an audit. There are so many legitimate expenses related to the operation of a home-based writing business, but many of them are overlooked. In order to hang on to your money, you need to utilize all of the deductions applicable. Were you aware that the cost of this book is a tax deduction? Be sure to save the receipt!

Accounting Methods

A business can be operated under one of three methods of accounting: cash, accrual, or hybrid. The IRS will be automatically informed of your choice when you file your first business tax return. If you decide you would like to change your accounting method, you will need to get approval from the IRS using Form 3115, *Application for Change in Accounting Method.*

Cash

Utilizing the cash method of accounting, business owners report income when it is actually received and expenses when they are actually paid. It is the most common and easiest method of accounting for your money. A check that you received or that was made available to you before the end of the tax year is considered income constructively received in that year, even if you do not cash the check or deposit it into your bank account until the following year. When you sign and mail the check you are using to pay for a business expense, it becomes an expense for the year in which you wrote the check.

Accrual

Operating under the accrual method, income must be reported as earned even when it has not been physically received. Expenses may be used to offset income, even when the actual payment has not yet been made. Under this method, accounts receivable and accounts payable must be maintained in order to determine these balances. These managerial reports will be explained later in this book. If you send a bill to a client for the editing work you completed, you must record the income at that point in time. When you receive an bill from the indexer you hired, that invoice represents an expense at the time of receipt.

Hybrid

The hybrid method offers a combination of cash and accrual systems. Most businesses will operate under cash or accrual, but this is another option for you.

Policies

It is important to convey your policies to your clients and subcontractors in a clear, understandable manner. The best way to handle this is to create written agreements or contracts.

For Clients

You may not have control over every aspect of the project. However, you will want to be sure certain areas are addressed in order to avoid questions or conflict when the completed project is turned in and payment is expected. It is important to note that late fees and finance charges should be stated in your legal agreements and on your invoices. Wording such as "Invoices not paid within 20 days of the due date are subject to a __% monthly finance charge," is recommended. Most of these charges are calculated as an Annual Percentage Rate (APR) then broken down into monthly fees. For example, an APR of 12% breaks down into a charge of 1% of the total due for each month the payment is past due. Rates between 12% and 15% are fairly standard, but state law varies so check the limits in your state before establishing your terms with a client. Consider the following when setting up agreements with clients:

- Services you will provide to them
- Method of delivery
- Deadline for the project
- Basis for payment such as by the word, hour, or project—most writers charge by the word or the project
- Number of revisions allowed
- You also want to include what rights you are selling and the limits of your liability
- Finance charges or late fees for payments not made according to your agreed upon terms

For Subcontractors

You may work with a transcriptionist, indexer, virtual assistant, or researcher in the process of completing the project. If you pay someone else to assist you, they become your subcontractor or employee. The IRS has strict definitions for making this determination which are explained later in the book. You will want to put the terms of this agreement in writing as well.

- Services you expect from them
- Method of delivery
- Deadline for project
- Basis for payment such as by the word, hour, or project
- Finance charges or late fees for payments not made according to your agreed upon terms
- Completed IRS Form W-9 so that you can complete IRS Form 1099-MISC (explained in more detail later in this book)

To maintain a professional image, you must be consistent and believe in the policies you set. Creating these contracts can also help you further define the scope of your services and provide a checklist to use as follow up during the project.

Here is a sample freelance writing contract you can present to a client. Remember that the contract needs to be customized for your use and based on the job you are completing. This is only an example.

Agreement for Freelance Writing Services

This agreement ("Agreement") is by and between _____ ("Client") of _____ _____ and _____("Writer") of _____ _____ for the sole purpose of completing the following projects collectively referred to as _____ ("Work"). The Agreement is entered into as of the _____ day of _____, 20XX.

IN CONSIDERATION OF THE MUTUAL COVENANTS MADE HEREIN, CLIENT AND WRITER AGREE TO THE FOLLOWING:

1. Description of Work: Writer agrees to produce Work as requested by Client and will deliver Work in printed copy to the Client address listed above and transmit electronic copy by e-mail to _____. Scope of Work includes:

_____

_____

2. Services and Compensation:

(a) Writer agrees to complete Work as defined in Section 1 in accordance with Client's request.

(b) Client agrees to pay Writer the compensation set forth in this Agreement as stated in Section 5 for the completed Work.

3. Representation and Warranties:

(a) Writer represents and warranties to the Client that all contributions of the Writer to the Work shall not infringe on the intellectual or other property rights of another party.

(b) Writer possesses full power and authority to enter into this Agreement, to fulfill obligations and to assign the rights assigned concerning the Work.

(c) Writer warranties sole authorship of the Work.

(d) Writer ensures reasonable care has been made to ensure that all facts and statements in the Work are true.

4. Confidentiality:

(a) Writer acknowledges confidential information ("Information") may be transmitted to and from Client for the purpose of completion of the Work.

(b) Writer will not, during or after the term of this Agreement, disclose any Client Information for any purpose.

5. Compensation:

(a) Client agrees to pay Writer $_____ (_____) on or before the due date defined as _____. Work shall be delivered to Client upon payment of fees and should include up to three (3) revisions.

(b) Client agrees that if requirements related to completion of the Work are changed, compensation may need to be adjusted. Should this occur, Writer will cease production of Work until new compensation is decided.

(c) Writer accepts payment in the form of check or money order.

(d) Writer shall perform the services to complete the Work as an independent contractor and bears the sole responsibility and obligation of payment of all local, city, state, and federal taxes related to completion of Work. Writer further understands that the Client is not responsible for unemployment insurance or workers' compensation premiums related to this Agreement. Writer has attached completed Form W-9 to this contract for Client's use.

(e) Cancellation of the Work must be written and delivered to Writer at the address listed on page 1. Upon cancellation, Client is responsible for payment of all expenses incurred and payment for Work completed to that point. The expenses will be determined by Writer based on the percentage of Work completed.

6. Rights and Acceptance:
(a) Writer assigns fully to the Client the Work and copyright and any intellectual property rights related to the Work.

(b) Client agrees to bear the cost of any financial requirements necessary to secure said rights.

(c) Writer agrees Client has the right to edit Work as deemed necessary for publication provided that the Writer is granted the right to review Work before publication.

(d) Client is responsible for written approval of Work prior to completion. Writer agrees to submit for written approval and Client agrees to accept responsibility for said approval. Writer is not responsible for errors occurring in this Work after Client acceptance of the Work.

7. Governing Law: This Agreement is governed by the laws of the state of _____.

8. Arbitration:
(a) Client and Writer agree that any dispute or controversy arising out of or relating to any interpretation of this Agreement or Work completed shall be settled by arbitration to be held in the state of _____ in accordance with the rules and legislation then in effect by the American Arbitration Association.

(b) The prevailing party in any arbitration or other legal action shall be entitled to receive reimbursement for all costs and expenses of such arbitration or legal action including but not limited to attorney's fees and expenses.

9. Entirety: This Agreement is the entire agreement between Client and Writer and supersedes any prior agreements between them with respect to this Work.

10. Severability: If any provision of this Agreement will be held to be invalid or unenforceable for any reason, the remaining provisions will continue to be valid and enforceable.

IN WITNESS WHEREOF, the parties hereto have executed this Agreement as of the day and year first written above.

WRITER   CLIENT
By_____   By _____
Printed Name: _____   Printed Name: _____

Here is a sample contract you can present to a subcontractor. Again, it needs to be customized for your specific use. This is only an example.

Subcontractor Agreement

This agreement ("Agreement") is by and between _____ ("Writer") of _____
_____ and _____ ("Subcontractor") of ____
_____ for the sole purpose of completing the following projects collectively referred
to as _____ ("Work"). The Agreement is entered into as of the _____ day of _____,
20XX.

IN CONSIDERATION OF THE MUTUAL COVENANTS MADE HEREIN, WRITER AND SUBCONTRACTOR
AGREE TO THE FOLLOWING:

1. Description of Work: Subcontractor agrees to produce Work as requested by Writer and will deliver Work by
_____ in printed copy to the written address listed above and transmit electronic copy by e-mail to _____
_____. Work is being completed for _____ ("Client"). Scope of Work
includes:

_____

_____

2. Services and Compensation:

(a) Subcontractor agrees to complete Work as defined in Section 1 in accordance with Writer's request.

(b) Writer agrees to pay Subcontractor the compensation set forth in this Agreement as stated in Section 5 for the
completed Work.

3. Representation and Warranties:

(a) Subcontractor represents and warranties to the Writer that all contributions of the Subcontractor to the Work shall
not infringe on the intellectual or other property rights of another party.

(b) Subcontractor possesses full power and authority to enter into this Agreement, to fulfill obligations and to assign
the rights assigned concerning the Work.

(c) Subcontractor warranties sole authorship of the Work.

(d) Subcontractor ensures reasonable care has been made to ensure that all facts and statements in the Work are
true.

4. Confidentiality:

(a) Subcontractor acknowledges confidential information ("Information") may be transmitted to and from Writer for
the purpose of completion of the Work.

(b) Subcontractor will not, during or after the term of this Agreement, disclose any Writer or Client Information for
any purpose.

5. Compensation:

(a) Writer agrees to pay Subcontractor $_____ (_____) within 30 days of completion
of Work. Work shall include as many revisions as is required to satisfy the quality and scope of Work defined by
Writer.

(b) Writer agrees that if requirements related to completion of the Work are changed, compensation may need to be adjusted. Should this occur, Writer will notify Subcontractor in writing and the terms of Compensation may be changed.

(c) Writer shall make payment to Subcontractor in the form of check or money order.

(d) Subcontractor shall perform the services to complete the Work as an independent contractor and bears the sole responsibility and obligation of payment of all local, city, state, and federal taxes related to completion of Work. Subcontractor further understands that neither Writer nor Client is responsible for unemployment insurance or workers' compensation premiums related to this Agreement. Subcontractor has attached completed Form W-9 for Writer's use.

(e) Cancellation of the Work must be written and delivered to Subcontractor at the address listed on page 1. Upon cancellation, Writer is responsible for payment of all expenses incurred and payment for Work completed to that point. The expenses will be determined by Writer based on the percentage of Work completed.

6. Rights and Acceptance:
(a) Subcontractor assigns fully to the Writer and Client the Work and copyright and any intellectual property rights related to the Work.

(b) Client agrees to bear the cost of any financial requirements necessary to secure said rights.

(c) Subcontractor agrees Writer has the right to edit Work as deemed necessary for publication.

7. Governing Law: This Agreement is governed by the laws of the state of _____.

8. Arbitration:
(a) Subcontractor and Writer agree that any dispute or controversy arising out of or relating to any interpretation of this Agreement or Work completed shall be settled by arbitration to be held in the state of _____ in accordance with the rules and legislation then in effect by the American Arbitration Association.

(b) The prevailing party in any arbitration or other legal action shall be entitled to receive reimbursement for all costs and expenses of such arbitration or legal action including but not limited to attorney's fees and expenses.

9. Entirety: This Agreement is the entire agreement between Subcontractor and Writer and supersedes any prior agreements between them with respect to this Work.

10. Severability: If any provision of this Agreement will be held to be invalid or unenforceable for any reason, the remaining provisions will continue to be valid and enforceable.

IN WITNESS WHEREOF, the parties hereto have executed this Agreement as of the day and year first written above.

SUBCONTRACTOR   WRITER
By_____   By _____
Printed Name: _____   Printed Name: _____

Advertising

There is a lot involved in establishing your business and getting that first customer, but it is only the beginning. You will need to build a solid client base for your writing business to succeed.

Consider hanging signs advertising your business on public bulletin boards with tear off phone number strips. Contact local newspapers to ask about writing a short column for readers where you can share tips on a topic you have researched in exchange for the publicity. For example, you may be able to write a column and instead of being paid by the newspaper, you are allowed to include your contact information which acts as an advertisement for your business.

Local radio stations may be interested in your tips for their listeners as well. If you are a sport fishing writer who can offer their listeners tips on great places to fish, pitch the tips to the station. You can record the tips and the station can air them with your name and contact information.

A Web site provides an affordable means to reach your customers 24 hours a day. Be sure to list contact information on every piece of promotional material you create.

Business cards and signs are a great way to let people know about your business. Hanging flyers at local colleges is a great way to attract professors looking for help writing their next article or book. Be sure to include all the benefits your service will provide and how it will make a positive difference in their lives. Keep your business cards handy so you can share them with people you meet who may have an interest in your services.

Networking is very important for any new business. Look into your local Chamber of Commerce or national writing organizations for additional people you can connect with or advertise through.

The Internet offers a multitude of ways to publicize, market, and promote your services as well as being a fantastic resource for learning more about the field of

Tips for Success

"I think that it is very important for a writer to find a niche. You've got to find an area in which you have expertise or experience that makes you stand out from others. It's also important to build a platform to create that expertise. Start with a blog, articles on Web site, maybe a Listmania list on Amazon, and build up to articles in national magazines. Eventually you will have created credentials for yourself in the area you've chosen and can possibly make the jump to selling a book on the subject."

Brette Sember, author of over 30 books, including the e-book *Writing and Selling Your Nonfiction Book Proposal* www.BretteSember.com

Ⓦⓡⓘⓣⓔⓡ'ⓢ Ⓑⓛⓞⓒⓚ

With all the Internet has to offer I would like to have a Web site for my writing business, but it can be really expensive to get a site designed and pay for all the hosting fees. If I decide to invest in the site, will it be a tax deduction?
— Aimee in New Hampshire

The Internet is a great place to advertise your writing business. You can deduct the purchase of your domain name, hosting fees, design, and site maintenance provided the Web site is used exclusively to promote your writing business.

writing. Connecting with organizations and other writers through the Internet is a productive way to spend a few hours each day. Many discussion groups are available to writers through Yahoo.com. Go to Yahoo's Groups link then enter "writing," "editing," or be even more specific and search for "moms who write comedy" or "science fiction screen play writers." You will be amazed by the number of writers who talk through these groups everyday.

Business or Hobby?

The IRS is vigilant about watching for taxpayers presenting an activity as a business when it is really a hobby. A hobby is an activity you pursue without expecting to make a taxable profit. You engage in the activity because you enjoy it. Income received from this activity needs to be reported, yet deductible expenses related to it are limited.

The IRS allows you to take business deductions only if you operate a real business. These deductions lower your taxable income so you pay less in taxes. The IRS will not allow you to deduct many expenses if your business is determined to be a hobby.

For example, a person may tell the IRS that their stamp collecting is a business so they can deduct some of the expenses. As a hobby, all of their income from selling the stamps is taxable. As a business, income can be offset by allowable expenses.

For years people tried to pass their hobby off as a business, but the IRS instituted new rules to stop this from happening. One rule was that in order for a business to be considered a business, it had to show a taxable profit during at least three out of the last five consecutive years. They also set perimeters such as the business must keep records and have some means of advertising such as business cards or letterhead. There are other factors to consider when distinguishing between a business and a hobby.

- Is the activity run in a businesslike manner? This includes having business letterhead, business cards, maintaining good records, and promoting your business through advertising.
- Do you depend on the income from the activity for your livelihood?
- Does the activity generate a profit in some years?
- Does the time and effort put into the activity indicate an intention to make a profit?
- Have methods of operation changed to improve profitability?

When determining whether you are carrying on an activity for profit, the IRS says all the facts are taken into account. No one factor alone is decisive. Keep these facts in mind when starting your writing business.

By understanding the recordkeeping basics involved in starting a business, preparing your federal income tax return will be easier. These basics serve as reminders that the decisions you make now will impact how you file your taxes later.

Chapter 2

Recording Income

It is a good idea to record all income received from your writing in one place. If you are using a computer program to make invoices for your clients or to track payments, it is still important to have a clear paper trail to follow.

When recording income you will need to list the date the funds were received, who has paid you, the amount paid, and the method of payment they used. You may want to note if they paid all that was owed to you or if there is still a balance due.

The people or companies paying you may require you to complete a Federal Form W-9 before making any payments to you. This is a simple form which asks for your name, address, and tax identification number.

During January of each year, you may also receive Federal Form 1099-MISC. This form is completed by the person or company paying you. A copy is then submitted to the Internal Revenue Service and to you as the recipient. This document reports your earnings from this payer. The dollar amount reported on the 1099-MISC should match the dollar amount you received from them. If the numbers do not match, call the payer to ask for a breakdown of their payments which you can compare to your records. If their numbers are wrong and you can prove it with deposited checks from them, notify the payer and they will file an amended 1099-MISC.

There are many different types of income that you as a writer and business owner may have. Being aware of these types of income will help prepare you for how each type needs to be recorded and tracked. The IRS deals with these types of income differently, which means it is important for you to understand how these incomes will affect your taxes.

Writing Income

You can earn money from writing a newspaper column, magazine article, Web site copy, grants, script writing, ghost writing, book royalties, and more. An advance you receive from writing a book is also considered income. This must all be reported as income even if you do not receive a Form 1099-MISC from the person or company paying you. It is a common misconception that if you do not receive a 1099- MISC, then it is not reportable income. To clarify, all income received from writing is taxable.

Tips for Success
"Hourly wage is king. Translate every project into how much money you make per hour of your time. Know how much your time is worth, have good tools for estimating how long a project will take you, and you'll never go wrong."

Rose Fox
Freelance Editor &
Journalist
www.
rosejasperfox.com

Bartering

In the eyes of the IRS, there are other forms of income which may be taxable to you as a writer and need to be recorded. One such form is bartering. Bartering is an exchange of property or services without involving the exchange of money.

The fair market value of property or services you receive in bartering should be included as income upon receipt. As a writer it may be hard to determine the fair market value of a newsletter you write for a flower shop in exchange for a bouquet of flowers. However, if both parties agree ahead of time to value the service, that value can be accepted as the fair market value unless the value can be shown otherwise. If you have not determined the value of the exchange, be sure do to so before this filing deadline.

Generally, the bartering value is consdered to be just like money you earn and should be tracked the same way. The income you receive from bartering is generally not subject to backup withholding unless certain criteria are met. Bartering transactions will normally be reported on Federal Form 1099-B, *Proceeds from Broker and Barter Exchange Transactions*. If you received a service or product through bartering, you should receive this form by January 31st of the following year. The dollar value reported here will need to be included on your Schedule C or other business federal tax form as income. The IRS does tend to scrutinize barter exchanges since the evaluation process is subjective.

Sale of Property

Another form of income we will discuss is from the sale of property. Just about anything you own personally or for your business can be considered a property. Personal property transfers may be taxable if there was a gain involved, but the IRS has deemed losses may not be tax deductible. Gains and losses from the transfer of business property is a reportable transaction and must be included on your tax return for the year the property was transferred.

In order to determine how much of the personal or business gain is taxable and how much of a business loss is tax deductible, the cost basis must be determined. In most situations, the cost basis is the amount you paid to purchase the property.

The cost basis can be adjusted to reflect additions (when the property increases in value) and deductions (when the property loses value).

Let's look at two types of property you can transfer.

Sale of Business Property

As a writer, it is common to purchase books for research to write articles, products for evaluation if you write product reviews, or equipment to use in your business. These items are considered business property.

As mentioned previously, a gain from the sale of business property may be considered taxable income and a loss from the sale of business property may be tax deductible.

A gain is defined as selling the property for more than it was originally purchased for. When the property sells for less than the purchase price, it is considered a loss.

What do you do with all the books, products, or equipment when the project is complete? Many people will sell them on eBay or Amazon, or to local resale shops for cash. As with many transactions, the IRS would like to take its share of this exchange as well. Many people do not realize the money they receive from these auctions and consignment sales may be taxable.

Let's say you purchased a series of books on Japan which were used as research for an article you completed on Japanese history for *National Geographic*. You paid $525.00 for the books the year you purchased them for your business. Since these books were allowable as a business deduction, you claimed $525.00 on your income taxes as an expense. This brings your cost basis from the original $525.00 down to zero since you used the cost to reduce your taxable income.

The books are listed on eBay and sold for $200.00. The IRS considers the dollar

Writer's Block

Each year software companies send me their latest and greatest electronic games for PlayStation for review. I play each game a few times then ask my niece and nephew to try the games as well. They are just the right age for this project. I record their comments and add them to my own then write the software review. The final document is published each month. As you can imagine, I have quite a few games by now. I can give some away to friends or relatives, but I have been thinking about selling some of these online. If I do this, will I have to report the sales?
—Sam in Idaho

Unfortunately, yes. In this situation, the products are given to you so the cost basis for you is zero. The copies that you give away are not a concern, but any that you sell can be considered taxable income. Be sure to record this money earned on your Monthly Income Form.

difference between your cost basis (now zero) and your sales price ($200.00) as a $325.00 taxable gain. This amount should be reported as income on your tax return. This is important because the cost of the books when you purchased them was classified as a business expense. Therefore the cost was deducted from your income and reduced your taxes. Since it was claimed as an expense, it must also be claimed as income when sold at a gain.

What if the books were given to you as review copies and you sell them to a local bookstore once your article is published? In this situation, the cost for you to obtain the books was zero, so the reportable income would be the actual amount you received from the bookstore. If it was given to you due to your business as a writer, you are required to report income from the sale of this business property on your business tax return.

Sale of Personal Property
Unfortunately, this rule does not follow through to the sale of personal property. What if you are a science writer, but you purchase romance novels for your own personal interest then sell them when you are done reading? This is considered a sale of personal property and may be subject to tax. If you realized a gain, tax is due; however, if you realized a loss, you cannot claim the deduction.

For example, you purchase a romance novel for personal reading and pay $5.95. You sell the book on eBay and receive a check from them for $6.95. The difference between what you paid for the book and what you sold it for was $1.00. This gain is something you should claim on your taxes. However, if you sold that same book for only $3.95, you may not deduct the $2.00 difference as a tax deduction since the transaction was personal.

Thankfully, the IRS does allow some leeway for personal investments. Instead of a romance novel, if this transaction was an item you held as an investment such as an antique coin or gem, your gains are still taxable, but any loss at the time of sale can be tax deductible.

Sales Tax
This will come up if you are selling books (or other tangible products) yourself. You will have to get a license from your state and look into any local tax liabilities, and then be authorized to charge, collect, and remit sales tax. The sales taxes you collect from customers are then turned over and paid to the government agency. The amount of tax you collect should equal the amount of tax you remit; therefore, sales tax is not considered a business expense or business income.

Special Consideration: Auction or Consignment Sales as Another Business
If your online auction sales are the Internet equivalent of an occasional garage sale, you generally do not have to report the sales. In a garage sale, you generally sell household items you purchased over the years and used personally. As long as you paid more for the items than you sell them for and are not in the auction business, the sales are not reportable. Losses on personal use property are not deductible, either.

If your online garage sale has turned into a business and you are purchasing items for resale with the intention of making a profit, you may have started an online auction business based on the IRS definition. Business income resulting from an auction or consignment sale is subject to taxes just like any other retail or service business. This income must be included as business income when it comes time to file your tax return.

Tracking Income

Now that you have read and understand what should be claimed as business income and what is considered personal income, we can start discussing the details of tracking income. A Monthly Income Form has been created for you to use. It is important to sit down on a regular basis and fill in this form. Once the monthly form is completed, be sure to carry the totals over to your Annual Income Form.

This method will give you an accurate picture of your sources of income and the information will be used to file your business tax return. Using this system, you will be able to track your income at a glance and will have a running balance of what you have earned to date each year.

Recording and tracking income is a necessary part of every business. There are so many different types of income, so it is important to understand how to record and file each type. When making bank deposits, be sure to itemize them in your checkbook register so that you can prove the income and can track the source. Detail is very important. Please feel free to copy the blank Monthly Income Form and the Annual Income Form in Chapter 10 for your use. You can view completed forms below from Write Now who uses the cash basis of accounting.

Tips for Success
"I use a spreadsheet to track all of my projects, invoices, and payments. I include all pertinent information such as contract numbers, ISBNs, due dates, and so on so that everything is visible at a glance."

Glenda Samples
Freelance Editor/Writer

Write Now
Monthly Income Form
For the Month of March

Date	Customer	Payment	Check
3/3	The Town Times	$110.00	1034
3/5	Good House	$85.00	67
3/6	City Reporter	$425.00	90321
3/15	Automotive Guide	$50.00	1037
3/18	State Street News	$45.00	428
3/25	State Street News	$45.00	434
3/28	Flower Power Magazine	$250.00	5356
3/29	Health Journal	$82.00	1089
3/29	State Street News	$45.00	439
	Total	$1137.00	

Write Now
Annual Income Form

Month	Income
January	$746.00
February	$1060.00
March	$1137.00
April	
May	
June	
July	
August	
September	
October	
November	
December	
Total	

Chapter 3

Business Expenses

Business expenses are the cost of operating a trade or business. These expenses are usually deductible if the business is working to make a profit. The more legitimate business expenses that you can document, the lower your taxable income will be.

Writers are able to realize some unique deductions which may be considered personal for most other taxpayers. For example, a book on Vermont used for researching your fiction manuscript which takes place in that state, tickets to a ballet used to build on a character you are writing about who is a ballerina, and even a DVD of a famous writer speaking about his or her skills which you can use for professional development may all be considered business expenses. Most writers will call expenses such as this research. However, writers need to be able to justify each expense, so be sure it is legitimate and you have the supporting documents to back up your claim.

Ordinary and Necessary

In any case, the Internal Revenue Service requires that your expenses be ordinary and necessary in order for them to be acceptable. An ordinary expense is defined as common and accepted in your industry and profession. A necessary expense means that you need to spend this money in order to operate the business. The expenses must not be considered extravagant, but an essential part of doing business.

It is important to differentiate between personal expenses and business expenses. Generally, you cannot deduct personal expenses. However, if you have an expense for something that is used partly for business and partly for personal purposes, divide the total cost between the business and personal parts. You can only deduct the business part as a business expense. Please keep in mind that in order for an expense to be deductible, it must be directly related to the operation of your business. Such expenses can include business recordkeeping supplies, professional training, and magazine subscriptions.

As a writer, you can work out of a home office, which is explained more in Chapter 4. You can also work in an office outside of your home. Depending on the actual location and use of the office, certain expenses such as utilities, can be deducted one of two ways.

If you have a home office, follow the instructions in Chapter 4 for deductions of a home-based office. If you have an outside office, be aware that you cannot have a tax deductible home office as well. It is one or the other. Fuel to heat this space, electricity to operate this space, and running water can be deducted as a direct expense for an outside office, or deducted as an indirect expense with a home-based office.

Possible Business Deductions

The following is a list of direct business expenses which may apply to your writing business. There are certainly other expenses which may arise in the operation of your business. These are provided as suggestions.

Accounting Services

Having a good bookkeeper, accountant, or financial expert to get your business records organized is recommended for any business. Depending on how your writing business is growing, you may want to hire someone to help with daily transactions or even someone who comes in once a month to prepare financial statements. By getting your records organized, you will find that tax preparation is less stressful and easier on your checkbook since you will not have to pay for the tax preparer to go through a shoebox searching for your receipts.

Advertising, Marketing, and Promotion

Ads in a newspaper, magazine, or on the radio promote your business. Advertising can include being a sponsor for a community or national event. Pens with your company logo can be considered advertising as well. Business cards, stationery, imprinted invoices, brochures, and flyers are other advertising mediums to consider. Authors may also deduct expenses paid to exhibit or display their product.

Agent Fees

The amount your agent deducts from any royalty checks is considered an expense to you. For example, your agent works out a deal with McGraw-Hill Publishing Company resulting in a $10,000.00 advance for a book you will write for them. Your agent's fee or commission is 10% of the advance; in this case, $1,000.00.

After the year is complete, McGraw-Hill will mail you a form 1099-MISC. This form lists the amount of money they have paid you during that year and will show the full $10,000.00. You will report the $10,000.00 on your tax return as income, but then you will report the $1,000.00 agent fee as a deduction leaving you with a net taxable amount of just $9,000.00.

Automobile Expenses

You can claim either the IRS Adjusted Mileage Allowance or the Actual Expense option for your business use of a personal vehicle. There are more details on this topic in Chapter 5, but in general you can track your miles and deduct the business portion of the use of your vehicle. Or, you can track the miles to form the percent of use then write off actual expenses used to maintain your car such as a portion of fuel costs and car insurance.

Bad Debt

It is a common misconception that people can write off bad debt. However, only under certain circumstances can bad debt be deducted. If you are using the accrual method of accounting, you may be able to write off bad debt. In this situation, the writer will invoice a client and, since it is the accrual method, record the money right away as income. If the client actually pays the invoice, bad debt is irrelevant. If the client does not ever pay, however, the amount billed can be written off as bad debt. This creates a deduction to offset the income and zeros out the transaction.

Most writers tend to use the cash method of accounting, so bad debt does not apply. In this method, the writer does not actually record the income until it has been paid. Therefore, there is no income to offset if the money is never paid because it was never counted as income in the first place.

Bank Charges

The fees that the bank pulls out of your business checking account are usually business expenses. This would include service charges, bank fees for per check processing and per deposit recording, and monthly charges. They also include fees for a check that bounced or overdraft protection fees. For this to be 100% deductible, the checking account must only be used for your business. If it is used for business and personal transactions, only the dollar amount that equates to the business percent can be deducted.

Books

You may want to purchase books on bookkeeping (such as this one) or books about your writing profession. Any publication including a magazine, newspaper, eBook, paperbacks, hard covers, journals, bound, and unbound titles can be tax deductible if they are somehow related to your business. As a travel writer, you may need to research a country. An author who creates cookbooks may need to purchase magazines with cooking ideas. Writers who work on Web site copy may need to learn a special Internet coding or language (i.e.: HTML, Java, C + +, PHP, BASIC) in order to create the best look online. Magazine subscription fees would also fall into this category.

Childcare

The expenses you pay for childcare while you are working can be a deductible expense provided the IRS guidelines are met. To qualify, you and your spouse (if applicable) would both have to be working or in the active pursuit of obtaining work and the child would have to qualify. The IRS defines an eligible child as one who is considered your dependent and is under the age of 13. There are special rules if custody of the child is shared as in a divorce. In general, only the custodial parent can claim this expense. If this situation applies, it is a good idea to consult instructions for IRS Form 2441 and reference IRS Publication 503, *Child and Dependent Care Expenses*. The IRS also provides a credit toward childcare expenses for qualified families. You can learn more about the credit in this publication as well.

Copyrights

A copyright can be obtained through the United States Copyright Office. Authors of a written book will download, print, and complete Form TX. The cost to file this form is $45.00 (prices can change though) and the payment must be sent with the completed form and 1–2 copies of the final copy of the book.

With works that have never been published, a single copy can be filed with the Copyright Office. For works that have been previously published, you must send them two copies. Once filed, it can take months for the copyright to process. When complete the office will send you a signed copy of the form you filed showing your copyright number as certification.

To deduct copyright fees, you will list the filing fee, postage or shipping to mail the copies to the copyright office, and the cost of making the actual book(s) that are sent. A copyright is an intangible asset—meaning it is not a physical item that can be touched. The certificate can be touched, but the rights it conveys cannot be. You will read more about intangible assets in Chapter 8.

Donations and Contributions

Donations or contributions that are not classified as gifts can also be tax deductible. Gifts are only deductible up to a certain amount which can change annually and are explained in more detail later on in this chapter. Donations of cash or property, however, are not subject to the gift limit. They have their own set of rules. Please note that there are new recordkeeping requirements for cash contributions. You cannot deduct a cash contribution, regardless of the amount, unless you have a written document such as communication from the recipient which contains the name of the charity, the date, and the dollar amount donated. The IRS only qualifies certain charities for this purpose including non-profit groups that are religious, literary, educational, or scientific in purpose. They also approve of charities that work to prevent abuse of children or animals. IRS Publication 526, *Charitable Contributions* offers a list of what is and is not acceptable for your donation to qualify as a tax deduction.

Education and Training

Conferences or conventions on writing, workshops to enhance your writing skills, DVDs you rent and watch for educational purposes, and classes you attend to learn more about a topic related to writing are all ways to benefit from this tax deductible expense. If you take correspondence courses, attend a college class or seminar specific to your industry, the tuition, registration fees, and in most cases your textbooks and supplies can be taken as a business expense.

Furniture

Your office desk, chair, file cabinets, tables, and bookcases for use or storage related to your business can all be deductible in some way. If you are using your office furniture for personal *and* business use, you may only be allowed to deduct a percentage of the furniture costs. (This will be discussed later in this chapter.)

Gifts

Each year writers can purchase gifts for people related to their writing business such as printers, publishers, agents, clients, and interviewers. You may purchase the gift in any dollar amount, but only $25.00 of the gift is tax deductible. If you purchase a fruit basket as a thank you for your agent and it cost $35.00, you can only deduct $25.00 of that cost as a business expense. The balance of $10.00 cannot be used to reduce your income taxes. Remember this is limited to $25.00 per person per year and the person must be connected to your business in some way for even the $25.00 to be deductible. This limit may be changed by the IRS at any time.

Insurance

There are many types of insurance which may apply to your writing business. As long as the insurance is related to the operation of your business, you may be able to deduct it as a business expense. Suggested insurance policies to consider include insurance that covers fire, theft, storm and accidents, medical and dental premiums as well as co-payments, liability insurance, credit insurance, workers' compensation, qualified long-term care insurance, automobile insurance, and business interruption insurance. If your business has elected to operate as an S-Corporation, certain restrictions for health insurance do apply. You can learn more about these restrictions with IRS Publication 535, *Business Expenses*. If you would like to obtain insurance, a call to your local Chamber of Commerce can help. Consulting your telephone book yellow pages are another option, but word of mouth referrals are the best way to find someone reputable.

Writer's Block

I have a friend who is a writer and says that since she needs to eat, all the food she consumes should be a tax deduction. I'm an editor; can I take this same deduction?
—Marcel in District of Columbia

Sorry, Marcel, your friend has been misinformed. Although we all can agree that eating is a necessary and ordinary part of being alive, it's not an acceptable business deduction. The IRS considers food for daily consumption a personal expense. Now some business related meals can be considered tax deductible and you will read all about those in Chapter 6.

Interest Paid Out

Interest paid on direct business expenses such as business loans, credit card loans, and store charges is 100% deductible as long as the item purchased is used exclusively for your business. Interest paid on a credit card that is used for both business and personal charges is not 100% deductible. In order to claim any of this interest, you will have to look at the original item charged then factor in the cost of that item and the interest rate applicable to only that item. Any interest charged on a personal purchase does not qualify as a business deduction.

Legal Fees

If you ask lawyers to review your book contract, or to draw up an agreement for working with a subcontractor, the fees they charge can be considered a business expense. You may also incur permit fees related to a home office or court fees related to collection of an overdue account.

Licenses, Dues, and Membership Fees

Licenses may be required by your town or state to operate a business in a home. The cost of your business license can be deducted as a business expense. Dues that you pay to local writing groups or organizations can also be considered deductible. Professional writers may belong to national writing groups who charge fees for membership or online forums for writers. As long as the organization or agency is related to your writing business, the membership fees can be deductible.

Maintenance and Labor

If you need to repair an office copier, the maintenance fee is 100% deductible. This would apply to repairs completed on any of your office equipment. Maintenance to get someone to mow your home lawn, however, is not deductible unless you have a qualified home office. In this situation a percent of the maintenance fee could be deducted. This is explained in more detail in the next chapter. Labor paid to someone outside of the family is deductible, but a wife who is a writer cannot pay her husband for the labor required to mow their home lawn even if she has an allowable home office. If they file a joint tax return, his labor is not deductible.

Meals and Entertainment

There are restrictions on these expenses which are explained in more detail in Chapter 6. In general, you may be able to write off 50% of these fees as a business expense provided you meet all of the requirements which define the meal or entertainment. For example, you arrange to meet your agent at a local restaurant for lunch and the purpose of the meeting is to discuss your newest book idea. This would qualify for the deduction. Now, if you were at a baseball game with your family, and your publisher walked by waving—your tickets to the event are not tax deductible. The main purpose and focus of the interaction must be related to your business in order to meet the restrictions connected to this expense.

Payroll

If you are considered an employer, you must register with the IRS and your state or local tax agencies. It will become your responsibility to pay wages, withhold taxes, match certain taxes and pay for others out of your business income. Processing payroll is a very detailed and time consuming project. Failure to deposit taxes by the deadlines can result in expensive penalties and fines. It is often suggested that you hire a payroll service to take care of this for you. However, if you want to do it yourself it is important that you obtain and understand IRS Publication 15 Circular E, *Employer's Tax Guide*. This publication provides information related to the federal payroll tax law. You will need to contact your state department of taxes to obtain information on local payroll requirements.

Phone Lines and Telecommunication

The IRS does not allow tax deductions for expenses related to your home phone line. The home line is considered to be the primary telephone line into your house and no deduction is allowed for this. If you add a new telephone line which is dedicated exclusively to business calls, you may deduct it as a business expense. If you add extra features to your home line such as call waiting and can prove they are essential to your business, you can deduct the cost of that add on. The main line, however, is still not deductible.

If you make a long distance business call on your home line, this is considered an add on and is deductible provided you can substantiate the call and that it is itemized with a separate charge on your phone bill. To substantiate the long distance call on your home phone line, write down on your daily planner or in a log of some sort who was called, the purpose of the call, the date, time, and duration of the call. Then, attach a copy of your phone bill with the long distance charge highlighted and keep it with your business records.

Monthly fees for a cell phone can be a business expense if used exclusively for business. If you use the phone for both personal and business reasons, you can deduct a percentage of the expense.

The percentage is determined by tracking total minutes on the phone each month. Highlight business calls on your cell phone invoice. Take the percent of time the phone was used for business and apply that to the total dollar amount of the bill and claim that as your deduction. As this book is being written, the IRS is analyzing this deduction and may change its deductibility.

Here is an example of how to determine the amount you can deduct from your cell phone bill. Let's say your cell phone bill for the month of March is $42.00 for 1000 minutes. You highlight the 500 minutes of calls on your cell phone bill which were business related. 500 business minutes divided by 1000 total minutes equals .50 which is 50%. In this situation, you can deduct 50% of your cell phone bill of $42.00 amounting to a deduction for March of $21.00.

Again, it is important to note this rule applies to your cell phone when used for both personal and business reasons. It does not apply to your main home phone line. You are not allowed to deduct any of those costs as a business deduction.

If you use a paging service for business, or make business calls from a payphone, the cost can be deductible. If you have to pay an office supply store such as Kinko's® in order to receive a business fax at their location, these fees are also deductible.

Postage and Shipping

Fees paid for stamps at the post office to mail a proposal, shipping fees paid to UPS, Federal Express, DHL, or any of the other carriers to transport something related to your business is deductible. The rental fee for postage meters can be deductible. The amount you pay to a delivery service to bring mail from your post office box to your office can also be a deductible expense.

Retirement Plans

As a writer opting to file as a sole proprietor or as an S-Corporation, you have some retirement plan options available. Requirements and tax savings for each plan are varied. I recommend you discuss your options with a financial planner or tap into the many online resources available to help with this decision. Some retirement plans to ask about include SEPs (Simplified Employee Pensions), Keogh, Solo 401(k), and Roth IRAs.

Writer's Block

I'm a freelance writer who is just starting out in the field working part time while I hold down full-time employment. I am not quite ready to make the leap to being self-employed. Should I be keeping track of my income and expenses even though I don't have a business license yet?
—Chelsea in California

Yes, Chelsea, even though you are working another job as an employee, your freelance writing will be considered self-employment and the income is reportable on your tax return. Since you have to report the income, it will reduce the tax you owe by also tracking your expenses.

State and local government may require you to obtain a business license, but taxes are due whether your writing is being done with or without the license.

Sales Tax

When purchasing an item to be used by your business, your charges may include local or state sales tax on the item. When state and local sales taxes paid are included in the cost of the item purchased they can be tracked as one expense. There is no need to separate the tax from the item cost.

Subcontractors

You may pay someone to work with you on a project, need to utilize an editor for your manuscript, or ask an indexer to work on your book. The relationship between you and this person must be investigated for classification. This person is either an employee or a subcontractor. The IRS will look at several factors before making this determination. These factors are explained in more detail in Chapter 7. If the person is determined to be an employee, you must withhold and match payroll taxes. This will require obtaining an IRS Employer Identification Number and normally a state business identification number. As a subcontractor, these payroll taxes will not be required.

Supplies

You can deduct computer supplies such as flash drives or CD ROMs, printer supplies such as toner and ribbon, office supplies such as folders, paper, labels, staples, pencils, tape, shipping bags, stackable trays, mailers, and paper clips as business expenses when used for business purposes.

Technology

Your computer, printer, monitor, mouse, and keyboard all qualify as business equipment when used for business purposes. Copiers, typewriters, dictation machines, label printers, calculators, PDAs, pagers, voicemail systems, modems, tape recorders, telephones, answering machines, wireless routers, laptop computers, and fax machines are examples of technology put into business use. If you have a business Web site, your hosting fees, domain name, Internet connection, and shopping cart fees are also deductible. Databases purchased related to your writing can be deducted as can fees paid for your e-mail accounts.

Utilities

If you have an office outside of the home, you can deduct 100% of the utility costs. This can include gas, water, electricity, and waste management. Remember, this is only applicable for offices outside of the home. When you have a home office, different rules apply and will be explained in the next chapter.

Keep Track of Your Business Expenses

These expenses should be recorded using the Monthly Direct Expense Form. Totals from each monthly expense form will be carried forward to the Annual Direct Expense Form and used for income tax preparation.

On the monthly form, record each transaction as its own line item and provide as much detail as possible. When you carry over totals to the annual form, you will put your own expense categories as headings at the top of each column to match your expenses for the month. You may not have the same columns used each month, but that is okay. Take a look at the sample forms from Write Now on the next page.

Tips for Success
"I'm able to stay organized because I set aside the first hour of every day to do administrative tasks for my business."

Amy Forstadt
Freelance
Communications and
Marketing Specialist

Write Now
Monthly Direct Expense Form
For the Month of April

Date	Check	Payee	Description	Amount
4/2	341	Bell Telephone	Office Telephone Bill	$235.72
4/2	342	Online News	Information/News Service	$82.59
4/4	343	Type for Us	Subcontractor Pay	$112.00
4/11	344	Bell Telephone	DSL fee	$45.88
4/18	345	Supply Depot	Paper	$13.40
4/25	346	The Town Times	Subscription	$73.50
4/28	347	Daily News	Advertisement	$218.00
		Total		$781.09

Write Now
Annual Direct Expense Form

January

Expense Category:	Telephone	Subcontractors	Advertising	Subscription	Supplies	Insurance	Total
Amount:	$167.89	$216.00	$75.90	$178.12	$353.58	$975.00	$1966.49

February

Expense Category:	Telephone	Subcontractors	Advertising	Subscription	Supplies		Total
Amount:	$112.90	$178.00	$25.00	$180.59	$69.96		$566.45

March

Expense Category:	Telephone	Subcontractors	Advertising	Supplies	Dues		Total
Amount:	$80.00	$285.75	$18.00	$94.67	$104.12		$582.54

April

Expense Category:	Telephone	Subcontractors	Advertising	Service/Subscription	Supplies	DSL	Total
Amount:	$235.72	$112.00	$218.00	$156.09	$13.40	$45.88	$781.09

Entertainment Expenses: $36.32

Start Up Expenses

In the past, if you happen to purchase business equipment prior to the opening of your writing business, it was referred to as a start up expense and special rules applied which required taxpayers to allocate (spread out) the expense over a specified number of years. The IRS is carrying out a congressional mandate tied to the American Jobs Creation Act of 2004 which makes it easier for businesses to deduct start up expenses paid or incurred after October 22, 2004. Under the new legislation, the IRS will allow up to $5000.00 (or actual costs, whichever is less) in first year start up expenses to be taken as a business expense in the year of purchase. Any amount not written off in the first year can be deducted over a period of 180 months starting the month after the business began.

It may be helpful to know how it used to work with start up expenses in order to understand how it currently works. In the past, start up expenses could not be deducted at all during the year they were incurred. If you spent a dollar before you started your business, you had to spread the dollar over several months—taking just a few cents of it as a deduction each time.

Now, the IRS is allowing you to deduct the expenses related to start up expenses in the same year you spend the money. If you spend $1.00 in 2008 as a start up expense (meaning before you are open for business) you can actually deduct that dollar from your taxable income in 2008. You no longer have to spread it out over several years taking just a few cents each year.

The IRS set caps on what you can actually deduct, however. Based on the most recent ruling, you can spend up to $5,000 on start up expenses, subject to limitations.

Two kinds of expenses qualify under this new deduction; money spent investigating whether to create or acquire a new business, and all business expenses incurred before the day your business started. The IRS cites the following expenses as allowable for this start up deduction:

- Advertisements announcing the opening of your business
- Compensation paid to employees for training required before business can start
- Costs associated with securing clients

Start up costs do not include any expenses which are otherwise deductible such as interest or taxes.

Reimbursed Expenses

As a writer, there are occasions when the company you are working for will cover some of your expenses. Since only one of you can deduct the expense, it is important to know who will be claiming it. Let's assume you are a travel writer and a magazine hires you to write an article about Paris, France. They agree to reimburse you for the cost of your flight and lodging, you pay the cost of your meals and transportation.

What can you claim against the income received from this project?

You can only claim what is not reimbursed by the magazine. Your meals and transportation are valid expenses which you paid and can be claimed as expenses on your tax return. You have paid for the flight and lodging with your own money, but then once you submit it to the magazine for reimbursement it becomes their expense. You cannot claim it as a tax deduction since the magazine is. You will record the cost of the flight and lodging in your records as a reimbursable expense. Once the magazine pays you, the money will be recorded in this same account so the net effect is zero change to your income and zero change to your expenses.

The Alternative Minimum Tax (AMT)

This controversial tax was enacted as part of the Tax Reform Act of 1969 to target wealthy people who were taking advantage of loopholes in the current tax code which allowed them to shelter some of their income. Because the rates were not adjusted for inflation, it now targets not only the rich but also the middle class.

This tax also comes into play when discussing expenses incurred by an employee that are not reimbursed or if a business owner is operating a mining or oil drilling business. The majority of writers do not have to be concerned about this tax. Despite a common misconception, it does not eliminate your ability to write off normal business expenses.

Depreciation

Some items that you purchase for your business will need to be depreciated. Depreciation is an income tax deduction that lets you recover a portion of the cost you paid for an asset over a number of years. It normally applies to items that are worth more than $100.00 and have a life expectancy of one year or more. The IRS has classifications and assigns a life to each class. In the eyes of the IRS for example, a computer is looked at differently than office supplies. A computer has a class life of several years and would need to be depreciated whereas the office supplies could be used up quickly and would be deducted in the year purchased.

The IRS requires us to amortize certain assets based on their class life and purpose. Some expenses can be deducted fully the year they are purchased. However, others need to be broken down into smaller dollar amounts and spread out over several years. The IRS determines the class life of just about every asset you could imagine. They share it all with us in IRS form 4562 instruction *Depreciation and Amortization* (Including information on Listed Property) and IRS Publication 946 *How to Depreciate Property*.

Utilizing the IRS approved methods for depreciation will still allow you to write off the entire dollar amount you spent (provided it is a deductible expense). It has to be done, however, over a predetermined period of years instead of taken entirely in the year it was purchased.

List Your Business Assets

To facilitate the depreciation process, you will need to create an inventory list of your business assets. Your inventory list should include:

1. A clear description of the item.
2. The date you purchased the item.
3. The date you placed it into business use.
4. The cost of the item.
5. Today's fair market value.
6. The percentage of business use. This is the amount of time the asset is used for your business.

This inventory list will be done once now, and then you will add to it when each new asset is acquired. When setting the fair market value, consider what you would be able to sell the item for on eBay or through your local newspaper. You will notice the value of some items will be the same as the cost. However, there may be times where the cost and value do not match. For example, you may be listing things now for the first time which were purchased and placed into use several months ago. The item may be damaged from months of use and not as valuable as when it was new. This would account for a discrepancy between cost and value. The IRS will also need to know the amount of time these assets are used for your business as opposed to being used by you personally. This business use is not connected to the business use percent used in Chapter 4 when calculating indirect home office deductions.

Determine Business Use Percentage
It can be tedious to determine your business use percentage of these items. No one expects you to complete a written log each time you are using a piece of equipment or office furniture. However, the IRS prefers documentation. Written proof can help you prove your business deduction was valid in the event of an audit.

If the time you spend working is fairly consistent, you can keep a written log for a week or two and record when you use each piece of equipment. Use this information to determine an average weekly use. Then convert it into a 12 month period to arrive at the total percent your business uses these assets.

If your time spent working fluctuates, you can consider tracking two weeks during a busy season and two weeks during a slow season. Determine the average time spent using the same method listed above.

If your use is exclusively business, there is no need to track time used for these assets since they would show 100% business use.

This inventory list would be used even if you do not have a home office. It is a list of everything of value to the business that costs more than $100 and is expected to last for more than one year. These items are considered assets to your business and you will need to report them on your tax return. Some items which may need to be depreciated include your computer, printer, fax machine, copier, software, desk, file cabinets, office chairs, carpet or other type of office flooring, bookcases, transcription machine, and your home if you have a home office. More information on claiming a home office deduction is shared in Chapter 4.

Here is an example of what an inventory list can look like. You will find a blank form for your use in Chapter 10.

Write Now
Inventory List

Description	Purchase Date	Business Use	Cost	Value	Business Use %
Copier	1/4/09	1/4/09	$358.00	$358.00	76%
Ink Jet	1/8/09	1/8/09	$225.00	$175.00	53%
Printer Computer	1/8/09	1/8/09	$557.00	$557.00	87%
Transcription Machine	2/5/09	2/5/09	$212.75	$190.00	100%

Section 179

There is one other option in considering how to recapture the cost of an item purchased for business use. There is a special IRS expense allowance called Section 179. The form for this is on the top portion of Federal Form 4562, *Depreciation and Amortization*. Basically, this option allows you to deduct up to a set dollar amount for the purchase of some very specific business items.

Normally, with long lasting and expensive items, you are required to depreciate the cost of the item over a number of years. This allows you to deduct a small portion of the item's cost each year you are in business. If the item qualifies, you can choose to utilize the Section 179 option and deduct the full cost of that item in the year of purchase. You may also choose to deduct only a portion of the cost of the item one year, and depreciate the balance over following years.

There are specific rules which must be followed to qualifying for this Section 179 deduction. It is best that you consult the instructions for this form to see if the item meets the requirements. One general rule is that the item you wish to expense with the Section 179 deduction must be tangible property (something you can see and touch) such as a computer or piece of equipment.

As a business owner, it is to your advantage to keep track of all of your business expenses so that you have a record of what purchases can be deducted from your income. Understanding what makes a purchase a legitimate business expense will help you know how the expense needs to be recorded and filed on your taxes.

Chapter 4

Business Use of Your Home

In addition to *direct* expenses, writing from a qualified home office can generate *indirect* expenses. The exact amount of this deduction is unique and determined by comparing the size of your home to the size of your office.

Claiming a Home Office Deduction

The Internal Revenue Service allows you to claim a home office deduction for the portion of the home used regularly and exclusively for business purposes. This should be your principal place of business or a place to meet with clients during the course of your day.

In determining whether an area is used regularly and exclusively, the IRS requires that absolutely no other activity occur in that area and no personal property is stored in that area. If you decide to use an extra bedroom in your home as your office, be sure to remove all non-business furniture and belongings from the room. This space must be used only for business, all of the time.

If your home office qualifies, the amount you can deduct as a business expense depends on the percentage of your home that you use for business. To determine this percent, you will need to compare your home to the amount of space in your home used for business. The two most common methods for compiling this information are square footage and the number of rooms in your house.

Square Footage

Take out the tape measure and walk around your house. Record the dimensions of your home and create a basic floor plan using these numbers. Multiply length by width to determine the total square footage of your house.

Next, record the dimensions of the space used exclusively as your home office. Again, length multiplied by width will give you the total square footage of your home office.

Compare these two numbers to arrive at the percent you can claim. Let's use an example of an 1800 square foot home with an office measuring 20' x 24'.

20' x 24' = 480 square feet
480 square foot home office ÷ 1800 square foot home =
0.2666; which can be rounded to 27%

Tips for Success
"My best advice is to focus. Don't allow anything to distract you. Find a place where you can work and as soon as you walk in, get to work. Don't accept any excuses from yourself. Right now, right here is your moment to write. Now, sit down and write!"

Margo Berman,
Speaker, Professor, Inventor
Author of *Street-Smart Advertising: How to Win the Battle of the Buzz and The Brains Behind Great Ad Campaigns*
www.
UnlockTheBlock.com

This means that 27% of the expenses you pay for your home, if the home office is only used for business purposes, may be deducted as business expenses on your tax return.

Rooms

If most of the rooms in your home are the same size, you can compare the number of rooms used by your home business to the total number of rooms in the house. An example using this option is listed below.

You have eight rooms in your home that are all about the same size. You use two of these rooms exclusively for business.

2 rooms used as a home office ÷ 8 rooms in the entire home = 0.25; or 25%

Now that you have arrived at the percent, you will be able to apply this to expenses which are related to the operation of your home and deduct them from your taxable income.

Some people are concerned that taking the home office deduction will trigger an IRS audit. My suggestion is to take the expense as long as you understand the guidelines for the home office deduction and meet the criteria. In the event of an audit, you will have done nothing wrong provided your home office is valid.

Indirect Expenses for a Home Office

Here are some suggested indirect expenses which may apply to your home office. Normally these are personal expenses and not deductible, but since you have a qualifying office in your home the IRS will allow you to deduct a percent of them from your taxable income:

- Electric bill for entire home
- Homeowner association fees
- Depreciation of your home
- Garbage removal/recycling fees
- Home heating/cooling
- Home insurance
- Mortgage interest or rent
- Painting—interior and exterior of home
- Property tax on home
- Repairs to your home
- Utility expenses
- Water/Sewer bill for your home

Writers may consider cable or satellite television as a necessary business expense. However, exercise caution when making this decision. The IRS has created Section 274 of the Internal Revenue Code to specifically address this issue. This portion of the law places strict limits on deductions for items which are "generally considered to constitute amusement, entertainment, or recreation." Such items are deductible only where there is a direct, clear tie to particular work.

Recording Indirect Expenses

Indirect expenses are very different from direct expenses. These involve separate care and attention because the entire dollar amount is usually not able to be deducted. Your indirect expenses should be recorded each month when you record your other business expenses and the forms are very similar to your Monthly Direct Expense Form.

The Indirect Monthly Expense Form is included in this book along with the Indirect Annual Expense Form. Sample forms have been completed for Write Now and blank forms can be found in Chapter 10 for your use.

Both of these forms will help you understand and keep track of the expenses you spend on your home that may qualify as a tax deduction. However, in order for any deduction to be made, your home office must be used strictly for business purposes. If it is used for personal and business reasons, you are not able to benefit from these deductions.

Write Now
Indirect Monthly Expense Form
The Month of February

Category	Monthly Expense
Electric	$156.00
Garbage/Recycling	$42.00
Home Heating	$217.83
Home Insurance	$56.00
Indirect Repairs	$0.00
Mortgage Interest/Rent	$893.84
Property Tax	$176.90
Water/Sewer	$93.00
Other:	
Total	$1635.57

Total Square Feet In Home	1800		Total Number of Rooms In Home	
		OR		
Total Square Feet In Home Office	480		Total Number of Rooms In Home Office	

Percent of Home Used by Home Office: 27%
This equates to 27% of allowable indirect expenses can be taken as a business expense to reduce your taxable income.

Write Now
Indirect Annual Expense Form

Month	Electric	Garbage/ Recycling	Heating	Insurance	Repairs	Mortgage Interest/Rent	Prop. Tax	Water/ Sewer	Other
Jan	125.67	42.00	226.78	56.00	12.07	893.17			
Feb	156.00	42.00	217.83	56.00		893.84	176.90	93.00	
March									
Apr									
May									
June									
July									
Aug									
Sept									
Oct									
Nov									
Dec									
Total									

Ⓦⓡⓘⓣⓔⓡ'ⓢ Ⓑⓛⓞⓒⓚ

My house is small so it's hard to find space to work. My sister suggested that I use my laundry room for an office by putting my desk in there on a table. There is already a washer and dryer in the room along with some racks for drying clothes and hampers. I would be cramped in the space, but would the IRS say this qualifies as a home office?
—Katherine in Virginia

In order for the space to qualify as a home office for a writer, it would need to be used only by you doing work related to your writing business. Since the laundry room is also being used for laundry, it does not qualify as a home office.

Chapter 5

Automobile Deductions

When you drive to interview someone for an article, to the library to do research, to an appointment with your publisher, to the store to get office supplies, or to the bookstore to purchase a book related to a project, you can track your mileage and produce a business deduction. The miles that you drive which are in any way related to the operation of your business, or the actual expenses required to maintain your automobile can be deducted from your income at tax time. This is one of the most overlooked tax deductions for writers. You will need to choose one method based on the options below.

Method 1—An IRS Adjusted Mileage Allowance

For the year of 2008, the rate is broken down into two parts. From January 1, 2008 – June 30, 2008 you can use 50.5 cents per mile. This rate increased to 58.5 cents per mile on July 1, 2008 and will remain there at least until December 31, 2008. This is normally adjusted annually. With this method you need to keep track of the miles you drive which are exclusively for business purposes.

On your Internal Revenue Service Adjusted Mileage Allowance Form you will need to record the date of the trip, your beginning odometer reading, the ending odometer reading, the total miles driven, your starting location, your destination, as well as define your purpose for the trip. You can see an example of this form on page 48.

It is a good idea to make copies of the form to be kept in your vehicle. Each time you use the vehicle for business purposes, just fill out the form. Be sure to save all completed forms with your other recordkeeping information. Another option would be to use your daily planner or calendar to track miles. When you write the appointment on your calendar, you can fill in the mileage information at the end of the day. This documentation is required to substantiate your deduction.

Method 2—The Actual Expense Deduction

To claim your automobile deduction with this method, you need to keep track of all receipts related to the operation of your business vehicle. You can include in this amount gasoline, oil, repairs, license, insurance, depreciation, parking fees, and tolls. You will need to note beginning and ending odometer miles annually to prove your deduction is valid.

If you are using one vehicle for both personal and business reasons you are only allowed to take a business deduction for the percent of the cost allocated to your business. For example, if you use your car 40% of the time for personal reasons and 60% of the time for business, you are only allowed to write off 60% of these actual expenses.

In this situation, even if you decide on Method 2, in order to determine your business percent you will need to track all miles driven on this vehicle. To do this, use the form provided for Method 1. Then indicate the purpose of your trip with a notation of business or personal. At the end of each form total up business miles then personal miles. At the end of the year, you will be able to determine the business percent.

It is important to note that the IRS has specific rules on this deduction. If you choose in your first year of business to use the Actual Expense method, you may not switch to the IRS Adjusted Mileage Allowance in a later year on that same vehicle.

If you choose IRS Adjusted Mileage Allowance in the first year of business, you lose the ability to take a great first year depreciation expense on your vehicle. The first year you put your vehicle into partial business use, you are able to benefit from the first year depreciation which is a considerable dollar amount. After that first year, the IRS considers the vehicle to depreciate at a slower rate.

It is possible, however, to switch from the IRS Adjusted Mileage Allowance method to the Actual Expense method and depreciate your vehicle with a smaller deduction using the straight-line method of depreciation. This is a way to calculate the depreciation of an asset. This method suggests that the asset, in this case, a car, will lose an equal amount of value for each year of its useful life.

Automobile Registration Form

Regardless of the method you choose, you need to fill out the Automobile Registration form. An example of this form is provided on page 48. This form will give your tax preparer valuable information related to your mileage deduction.

The top of this form should be filled out right away with regards to name, make, model, year of vehicle, year placed into business use, and beginning miles for the year. The number recorded as the ending miles is based on the total miles driven for the year and will have to be completed on or after December 31st each year.

Once you fill out the mileage form in your vehicle, you need to record the beginning point and ending point, or period of time the vehicle was in use. The period of time may be on a weekly or monthly basis. The period of time you choose to include depends on which works best for your situation. Include the total mileage for the period of time using the bottom portion of this Automobile Registration form. If you are using the IRS Adjusted Mileage Allowance Method, simply list your beginning odometer reading as of January 1st and your ending odometer reading as of December 31st. On the Business Mileage line, enter the total miles recorded on your monthly table on the bottom half of the form. Personal mileage, if any, would be the difference.

If you are using the Actual Expense method for your automobile deductions, fill in the same information and be sure to record your monthly vehicle expenses in the column provided.

If you are using the Adjusted Mileage rate option, record the total monthly mileage rate deduction (miles for the period of time multiplied by the rate). If you are using the second option of Actual Expenses, add up the total actual automobile expenses on your Monthly Direct Expense Form. In order to track the deduction, make sure you include all of the expenses for the appropriate period of time.

Which Method Is Best for You?

You may still be uncertain which method is best for you and your writing business. The IRS Adjusted Mileage Allowance gives you a rate (50.5 cents 1/1/08–6/30/08 and 58.5 cents 7/1/08–12/31/08) per mile for business miles traveled. The Actual Expense deduction allows you to expense a defined percentage of certain (not all) expenses related to your vehicle.

If you have a new vehicle, or one that is very reliable and not in need of many repairs, the Actual Expense method may not generate as much of a tax deduction as the IRS Adjusted Mileage Rate. On the other hand, if you have an old car that is always in need of repairs, the Actual Expense method may be a better option.

The IRS Adjusted Mileage method does not require you to keep track of any receipts. You only have to keep a record of your mileage. The other method requires receipts which may be challenging and less desirable for some people.

Regardless of which method you choose, you should keep track of everything in the first year a vehicle is put into business use. This way, you will have a record of your expenses and be able to choose which method generates the biggest tax deduction.

Suggestions of often overlooked business related mileage for a writer can include travel from one client to another to conduct an interview or research, miles driven to purchase job supplies, travel for out of town business trips and professional meetings as well as to classes or college courses related to your writing career.

Writer's Block

As a writer working from my home office, I don't put many miles on my car. I think it was only 5,000 total miles last year and of that only about 1% was business. Can I still take this as a tax deduction?
—Jake in Texas

Yes, even when the car is not driven often, you can deduct your business mileage as an expense provided you have a written log to substantiate your claim. As much as it can be a bother to record mileage, it is required in order to claim the tax deduction.

Write Now had selected Method 1 and completed forms are filled out on this page for your review. The automobile expense forms can be found in Chapter 10.

Method 1
IRS Adjusted Mileage Allowance Form
Business Use Only For the Period of: April 1 - 30

Date	Beginning Odometer	Ending Odometer	Total	From	To	Purpose
4/2	343	358	15	Home	Library	Research Japan Project
4/2	358	412	54	Library	Senior Center	Interview for Japan Project

Total Business Miles This Period	69
Previous Business Miles	92
Year to Date Business Miles	161

Automobile Registration Form	
Make	Nissan
Model	Sentra
Year of Manufacture	2008
Year Placed in Business Use	2008
Beginning Miles – January 1, 2008	251
Business Miles	
Personal Miles	
Ending Miles – December 31, 2008	

Annual Summary

Month	Personal Miles	Business Miles	Automobile Expenses
January		42	
February		38	
March		12	
April		69	
May			
June			
July			
August			
September			
October			
November			
December			
Total			

Chapter 6

Entertainment & Travel

Deducting entertainment and travel expenses can be tricky. It is important to make sure these expenses are necessary for your business. Otherwise, they may be considered a personal (not deductible), rather than a business (deductible) expense.

Entertainment Expenses

You may be able to deduct business related entertainment expenses for entertaining an agent, fellow writer, or someone directly related to your writing business. These entertainment expenses can include meals, tips, and recreational events. However, in most circumstances, the amount you can deduct is limited to 50% of the actual unreimbursed costs. The IRS is considering an increase in this amount to allow 80% reimbursement. As of this printing, the deduction has not been raised, but be sure to visit the IRS Web site for updates.

Determine the Purpose of the Expense

In order for an entertainment expense to qualify as a deduction, you must determine the purpose of the expense. As mentioned in Chapter 3, in order to claim any expense, it must be ordinary and necessary for your business. If any cost is considered lavish or extravagant, you will not be allowed to deduct that expense.

It is important to actively engage in business related discussion or activity during this meal or event. Inviting a client to lunch to discuss how you can improve the look of his or her Web site by updating the content would be a justifiable expense. It would also be acceptable to take a subcontractor to dinner to discuss the work he or she does for you, have lunch with your agent to discuss a new proposal, and meet with your publisher about your newest book release. The key is that the primary purpose of the meeting must be business related and the discussion must focus on business.

Understanding How Unreimbursed Costs Work

Unreimbursed costs are important to understand because only 50% of the actual amount can be deducted. Many people, both self-employed and employees, will submit meals and entertainment costs to a client or employer for reimbursement. Unreimbursed costs can show up on an invoice from a self-employed person to the company they are working for. It can also show up as an expense report submitted by an employee to their employer.

If the person claiming the tax deduction submits the receipts to another party who then pays the total expense, the expense becomes deductible to the person or company actually covering the cost.

For example, you are a writer working as a subcontractor for a small publishing business. You take a fellow writer out to lunch to discuss something you both plan to work on for the publishing company. You pay for the meal. Therefore, you can claim 50% of that bill on your self-employment tax return. However, you may also be able to submit the receipt to the publishing business you are working with and ask to be reimbursed. If the publisher reimburses you 100%, your net cash out of pocket is zero because you have been reimbursed for the total amount of the bill.

You will also not be able to file this expense on your taxes because you have been reimbursed 100%. The publisher, however, would then claim the cost of your meal on his or her taxes and be able to deduct 50% of what he or she paid you.

Some companies have a policy that caps what they will reimburse you for a business meal. For example, let's say the cap is $25.00 for lunch. That is the most the company will reimburse you, regardless of what you spend. The bill for your lunch with your fellow writer ended up being $60.00. You submit your receipt to the publishing company. They will reimburse you $25.00. This makes your unreimbursed expense for your meal $35.00 ($60 - $25). This means you can report only $35.00 as an expense on your self-employment tax return. You will be able to deduct 50% of the $35.00, equaling $17.50.

Keep Track of the Entertainment Expenses

It is a good idea to keep a written log of your entertainment expenses. Be sure to fill in as much detail as possible and you should attach receipts to the form unless you are using the Standard Meal Allowance discussed later in this chapter. A written log of your expenses provides the documentation required by the Internal Revenue Service to claim the deduction. Since entertainment expenses are not fully deductible, record these in an Entertainment Log at the bottom of your Monthly Direct Expense Form, outside of the table, then carry the totals forward to a similar location on your Annual Direct Expense Form. A form is completed for you to review and a blank form can be found in Chapter 10.

Write Now
Entertainment Log
For the Period of July 1 - 31

Date	Location	Purpose	Amount
7/1	Café Latte	Meet with Mrs. Gray of Jones & Co to review terms of writing assignment on company history	$45.78
7/13	Lunch Express	Meet with Liz Williams regarding my bid for rewriting her Web site copy	$38.99

Travel Expenses

When traveling away from your home overnight for business related purposes, you can claim many business deductions provided the appropriate paperwork is maintained. The IRS defines overnight as being gone substantially longer than a day's work or long enough to require the need for sleep or rest to meet the needs of your work while away from home.

You can include the cost of transportation (plane, bus, train, car, etc.) between your home and the business related destination. If you choose not to rent a car, you can also deduct taxi or subway fees to move within this new location in order to conduct business. Traveling to conferences, training courses, and seminars are common in the writing business. Other traveling is acceptable provided it can be substantiated as necessary for your business.

Lodging costs can be deducted if your trip is overnight or long enough that it would be reasonable to require rest. Payment for sending faxes or computer use fees from a hotel are also considered reasonable. You can deduct the cost of laundry or dry cleaning while you are on this trip as well.

Meals While Traveling

Meals while traveling are still 50% deductible, but you have two options to choose from when expensing them: Actual Costs or Standard Meal Allowance.

Option 1: Actual Cost

When determining how to record travel expenses, you have two options. The first involves keeping track of the actual costs you incurred. As mentioned earlier, you can only deduct 50% of unreimbursed expenses. This method also requires you to keep a record of the costs to submit with your taxes.

Option 2: Standard Meal Allowance

You have another option to choose from, however. This is called the Standard Meal Allowance. This option allows you to expense a standard amount which is determined by geographical location. The IRS has determined the average cost of meals and lodging for most cities within the United States and refers to this as a Per Diem Standard. The rates are normally adjusted annually and can be found on the IRS Web site. You find the city, town, and/or state you are incurring the expenses in, and then see what the IRS will offer as an allowance for that area. This option is available only if you are within the continental United States.

With the Standard Meal Allowance method, you do not have to keep receipts from meals as proof. You still have to prove the time, place, and business purpose of your travel. With this option, you have two areas of allowances you can work with (1) daily meals and (2) incidentals. Incidentals are miscellaneous expenses such as tips to a baggage carrier or the transportation between places of lodging and business. When traveling, your meals can be expensed one of two ways, provided you prove your purpose was for business. You can use all of your actual receipts or use the dollar amount the IRS allows for the geographical location of your travel.

Vacation Versus Business

Sometimes a business trip may lead to an opportunity for a vacation. For example, if a writer from California is asked to do a two day book signing in New York City and decides to bring her family along, the expenses related to the writer are deductible. However, no portion of the family expenses can be deducted.

In this same situation, let's assume the writer extended her trip to a full week so her family could see a Broadway show and visit some museums. Will the costs be deductible? The percent of the expenses attributed to the author for the book signing are still 100% deductible. The rest of the trip will be a vacation and therefore cannot be considered a tax deduction.

Since we can assume the writer took a plane from California to New York, how would she expense her one plane ticket used for business and personal reasons? She will need to determine the percent of her time used for business and record only that portion. For example, let's say the ticket cost $600.00. She was gone six days. Two of the days were connected to the book signing and four of the days she spent with her family on vacation. In this scenario, the IRS would allow her to claim $200.00 (one third) of her $600.00 ticket as a business expense because she spent one third of the trip doing business.

The following completed form is an example that can help you document a travel deduction. Be sure to attach all receipts to this log and record totals on your Monthly Direct Expense Form.

Travel and entertainment costs are similar to the usual and regular business expenses in that you must prove the costs are necessary to your business. Keep in mind that in some situations the expenses are deductible, but in others, they are not. Similar to any business expense, these costs need to be tracked and recorded carefully in order to easily determine how much, if any, of the expense can be deducted.

Write Now
Travel Log
For the period of August 1 - 31

Date	Location	Purpose	Amount
8/7	Up High Airways	Travel to New York to attend editor conference	$414.75
8/7	Taxi	From airport to hotel	$23.00
8/7	You Sleep Inn	Lodging – 2 nights for 2 day conference	$785.00
8/9	Taxi	From hotel to airport	$23.00

Chapter 7

Employee Versus Subcontractor

As your writing business grows, there may be times when you need to hire help. The Internal Revenue Service has strict definitions they use when determining if a person working for your business is an employee or a subcontractor. If this person is an employee, you will be responsible to withhold, match, and remit certain taxes. If the person is truly a subcontractor, you are generally not liable for these taxes.

How to Set up Subcontractors

For contractors, you need to supply Form W-9 from the IRS for them to complete and return to you. This form is used to convey their name, tax identification number, and mailing address. You will use this to complete a Form 1099-MISC if you pay them over $600.00 (based on 2008 tax law) during the course of a calendar year. Please note that Form 1096 is required as a cover sheet when 1099-MISC is filed. These forms can be ordered through the IRS Web site.

If you do not complete the 1099-MISC, the IRS has the option of not allowing any expenses related to this subcontractor. They want to be able to connect your expense for this subcontractor as reported on a 1099-MISC to this subcontractor's income reported on their Schedule C or other tax form.

Since some subcontractors may not realize the tax implications of receiving money from you on the form 1099-MISC, the IRS is hoping they will help the agency track down businesses that misclassify them. Your subcontractors will have to report earnings just as you do and will be subject to similar taxes.

If the subcontractor decides to question your classification, they can file Form 8919, *Uncollected Social Security and Medicare Tax on Wages*, and ask the IRS to investigate their status with you. If they decide you have misclassified the subcontractor, you can be held liable for payroll taxes and be required to treat this person as an employee.

It is a good idea to obtain the completed W-9 before issuing any checks to the subcontractor. If, for some reason, they refuse to provide the information, the IRS may not allow you to claim the expense.

Tips for Success
"Connect with others in the industry. Writing is a lonely profession and writers are vulnerable to feelings of isolation. Get connected through online writers groups, go to conferences, join social networks, and work at building relationships with colleagues."

Brenda Nixon, M.A. Author of *The Birth to Five Book* and National Speaker
www.BrendaNixon.com

How to Set up Employees

If the person helping you is determined to be an employee, you will need to provide a W-4 and I-9 to be completed before hiring, then withhold and match employment taxes. Monthly, quarterly, and annual payroll tax forms may also have to be filed with your state and the IRS.

Determine the Difference

The following information is from the IRS Publication 15-A *Employer's Supplemental Tax Guide* and will help you make the determination between a subcontractor and employee. To determine whether a worker is a subcontractor or an employee, you must examine the relationship between the worker and the business. All evidence of control and independence in this relationship should be considered. The facts that provide this evidence fall into three categories—Behavioral Control, Financial Control, and the Type of Relationship itself.

Behavioral Control

This covers facts that show whether the business has a right to direct and control how the work is done, through instructions, training, or other means. For example, a business usually instructs an employee how, when, and where to work. The following are examples of types of instructions about how to do work.

- The time and place the work needs to be done.
- The tools or equipment that should be used.
- The workers that need to be hired to complete or assist with the work.
- The location where supplies and services should be purchased.
- The work that has to be performed by a specified individual.
- The order or sequence that should be followed when completing the work.

Different jobs will require different amounts of instruction. An employer may not give many instructions, but he or she may still have behavioral control over how the results of the work are completed.

Financial Control

Financial Control covers facts that show whether the employer or business has a right to control the business aspects of the worker's job. This includes:

Writer's Block

I'm a self-employed political writer and frequently interview politicians over lunch and pay for the meal. Are the costs of these meals deductions for me?
—Max in Kansas

If the interview is related to your writing and you keep a written record to document what was discussed and who was with you, the answer would be yes.

- *The extent to which the worker has unreimbursed business expenses.* Most employees are reimbursed for business expenses. For example, they purchase office supplies with their own funds, submit a receipt to their employer and are reimbursed. Subcontractors are usually required to pay for their own supplies. When they purchase paper at an office supply store, they pay for it with their own funds. It is considered one of the many costs related to operating their business.
- *The extent of the worker's investment in the business.* Employees, for instance, do not normally need to invest funds in the company they are working for. They arrive at work, do their required tasks, leave work and at the end of the period are paid for their time. Subcontractors normally do have to invest their own funds or obtain loans in order to secure funding to get the business started. In this situation, the person would have made an investment in the business.
- *The extent to which the worker makes services available to the relevant market.* A subcontractor offers a service or product to the public. They may start with one customer or one client, but the intention is to grow their business and expand into the market. Employees generally work for one company and do not make their services or products available to other companies.
- *How the business pays the worker.* A subcontractor is generally paid on a per project basis, although some exceptions exist. An employee however, is usually guaranteed hourly or weekly wages. Subcontractors need to provide a service or product to a customer or client. Generally they will create an invoice or bill to document this transaction and submit it for payment. The company will pay the subcontractor the agreed upon or invoiced fee. An employee, however, is hired by a company. They do not submit an invoice to their employer. Another distinction is that employees are given Federal Form W2 to show their wages earned and taxes withheld. Subcontractors may not be paid as employees or have payroll taxes withheld. Their earnings are reported on a Federal Form 1099-MISC.

Writer's Block

There is an indexer in town who runs her own business. I hire her to do all the indexes for my books. Other people hire her to do this as well. Would the IRS tell me she's an employee or a subcontractor?
—Sarah in Nevada

Based on the information you provided, I would think she is working as a subcontractor for you and for all the people she completes indexes for. The key points in your question that led me to this determination was that she runs a business and she provides a service (indexing) to more than one customer. I suggest you ask her to complete the W-9 and send her a 1099-MISC as warranted.

- *The extent to which the worker can realize a profit or incur a loss.* For example, employees do their assigned tasks and are paid for their work. They always earn money. Subcontractors, on the other hand, may earn money from a particular job, but they can also lose money. They may under bid a project, have accidents occur on the job which they have to pay for, and may make mistakes that they have to rectify at their own expense. Subcontractors can lose money by spending more than they earn on a job or project.

Type of Relationship

Facts that show the type of relationship between the business and the worker include:

- Written contracts describing the relationship the parties intended to create.
- The extent to which the worker is available to perform services for other, similar businesses.
- Whether the business provides the worker with employee-type benefits, such as insurance, a pension plan, vacation pay, or sick pay.
- The permanency of the relationship.

A general rule is that you, the payer, have the right to control or direct only the result of the work done by a subcontractor and not the means and methods of accomplishing the result. Anyone who performs services for you is your employee if you can control what will be done and how it will be done.

If you incorrectly classify an employee as a subcontractor, you can be held liable for employment taxes for that worker plus a penalty. If you want the IRS to determine whether a worker is an employee, file Form SS-8 *Determination of Worker Status for Purposes of Federal Employment Taxes and Income Tax Withholding.*

Writer's Block

What percentage of my income should I set aside for taxes? I've always heard 50%, but have no clue if that's accurate or not.
—Tricia in California

Unfortunately there is no set percent that works for everyone. As a self-employed writer your income will be combined with all other family income. Your writing expenses will also be combined with federal income tax deductions based on total income as well as the number of dependents you have and your filing status. The best way to get the most accurate percentage to set aside is to visit the IRS Web site and complete form 1040ES. This form will guide you through a series of questions and help you determine what is right for your family.

In general, I would say 50% is much more than most people would have to set aside.

Chapter 8

Business Management

There is so much involved in running a business and, at times, it can be hard to juggle everything. By reading this book you have taken a positive step toward ensuring the success of your business and have learned the importance of good recordkeeping. However, you may still be wondering how important it is to track these numbers and how knowing these numbers will really help your business.

Managing the financial aspects of your business is very important. The numbers we have been tracking create a financial picture and understanding this picture will help you with budgeting as well as planning.

Management Reporting

There are many financial reports you can create which will show how much money your business has earned and where it is going. These reports are essential to providing you with a clear picture of what is happening in your business. We will discuss a few of these reports in this book including a Profit and Loss Statement, Balance Sheet, Income Projections, Accounts Receivable Summary, and Accounts Payable Summary.

As a writer, you may want to know how much money you earned each month and how much you spent. The Profit and Loss Statement will give you that information. The Accounts Receivable Summary will track how much your customer owes you and when the payment is due. The Accounts Payable Summary will track how much money you owe to others and give you all the information you need to stay within your budget.

Profit and Loss Statement

One of the most valuable financial reports is called a Profit and Loss Statement. It is also referred to as an Income Statement since it shows how much money you have earned and how much has been spent during a defined period. This report is commonly created on a monthly basis. It can be used with either the cash or accrual method of accounting.

You will need to record all sources of income and expenses for the period on this report. Utilize your Monthly Income Forms to determine income and your Monthly

Tips for Success
"Write at the same time every week. I wrote early Saturday and Sunday mornings. It also helped that I had a little checklist of the parts of the books that I needed to write. I'd look at the list and choose a part that seemed motivating for me to jump into. Then, when I finished it, I'd check it off the list. Very rewarding!"

Katy Piotrowski, M.Ed. Author of *The Career Coward's Guides* www. careersolutionsgroup.net

Direct Expense Forms to determine expenses. You will also need to record totals from your Indirect Monthly Expense Forms using the business percent to generate a final dollar amount.

The net profit or loss revealed by this report will enable you to make more informed business decisions. If you are consistently showing a loss, you may need to consider if you are charging enough for your services. If you are showing a profit, be sure to use this information when calculating your federal estimated tax payments to help you avoid a penalty for underpayment. A sample Profit and Loss Statement is included for your review and a blank form is included in Chapter 10 for your use.

Write Now
Profit and Loss Statement
For the Period of: June 1- 30

Income:	Amount	Total
The Town Times	300.00	
Automotive Guide	125.00	
State Street News	75.00	
Total Writing Income		$500.00
Other Income:	**Amount**	**Total**
Bank Income	8.00	
Total Other Income		$8.00
Total Income		$508.00
Expenses: Direct	**Amount**	**Total**
Telephone	103.35	
Training	18.00	
Supplies	41.30	
Subscription	12.75	
Total Direct Expenses		$175.40
Expenses: Indirect (27% of total)	**Amount**	**Total**
Electricity	21.32	
Mortgage Interest	195.78	
Recycling	5.37	
Total Indirect Expenses		$222.47
Total Expenses		$397.87
Profit or Loss		$110.13 Profit

Accounts Receivable and Accounts Payable Aging Summary
As mentioned earlier in this book when you utilize the accrual basis of accounting, income is counted as it is earned—not when it is physically received. Using this method also means that expenses are considered when they are incurred rather than when they are actually paid.

In order to track income and expenses using the accrual basis, you will need to create a billing system which utilizes Accounts Receivable and Accounts Payable Summaries. A summary is simply a list of the clients you have billed and vendors you need to pay. These summaries are taken a step further, and are used with an aging system. The summaries are usually run weekly or monthly. Samples of each report are provided on page 60 along with blank forms in Chapter 10.

Accounts Receivable Aging Summary
An Accounts Receivable Aging Summary can show you how much money is owed to you and when it should arrive. For example, imagine that you write an article for a newspaper and submit an invoice for your work. You put the date on the invoice. On the Accounts Receivable Summary you consider the date you created the invoice, which company you created it for, and how much they owe you. The balance due at this point will go in the Current column (see Sample of Accounts Receivable Summary on page 60).

If your invoice was due within 30 days and 30 days has passed without payment, you will move this client over into the Past Due column(s). See the City Press row in the Accounts Receivable Summary as an example. It is not uncommon for writers to work on more than one project for the same client. This is the case with City Press. The example shows two different jobs, billed at two different times, on two different invoices, with two different due dates. One job was completed and billed out for $210.00. The date of the example summary is July 1–5. Let's assume payment was due within 30 days of the invoice date. The invoice for $210.00 was sent on June 2nd. Payment was due on or before July 2nd. It is now the week of July 1–5 and payment has not been received. The payment is now past due, so the amount shifts to the Past Due 1–10 Days column.

You completed a second project for City Press and invoiced $100 on June 30th. This payment is not due until July 30th. The dollar amount due for this job goes in the Current column because payment is not past due.

It is important to carry this past due payment forward so that you know how much money will be coming in for work you billed out. It helps with budgeting when you are self-employed and it also reminds you regularly which clients pay their bills on time and which ones take weeks or even months to send payment. The next time an assignment is offered, you can refer to this summary to remind you how the client treated your payment in the past. You may want to ask for prepayment or tell them you are not interested since there is a long delay in receiving your payment.

It is usually a good business decision to not do new work for a client once they get too far past the due date. Some aging reports work with Current, 30 Days Past Due, 60 Days Past Due, etc. You can change the range of days past due to fit your needs for your business.

Accounts Payable Aging Summary
The aging system works in a similar fashion for the Accounts Payable summaries. On this side of the equation, you are the one paying the bills. For example, let's say your business has an account at Office Supply Central and you go there on July 2nd to purchase a $125 case of paper. In the Current column for the July summary,

you would write $125. If you were unable to pay this bill, the next time you work on your finances in July you will record the $125 in the Past Due 1–10 Days column. This process will allow you to keep tabs on how much money you owe so you can budget your money to pay it off.

Write Now
Accounts Receivable Summary
For the Period of July 1-5

Source	Current	Past Due 1-10 Days	Past Due 11-20 Days	Past Due 21+ Days
City Press	$100.00	$210.00		
Home and Houses	$575.00			
Quill Digest	$50.00	$200.00		
Meadow Books	$100.00	$100.00		
Times Journal	$50.00		$50.00	
Total	$875.00	$510.00	$50.00	$0.00

Write Now
Accounts Payable Summary
For the Period of July 1-5

Payee	Current	Past Due 1-10 Days	Past Due 11-20 Days	Past Due 21+ Days
Office Central	$125.00			
Daily News	$45.28			
Type For Us	$735.61			
Bell Telephone		$120.00		
Online News		$76.83		
Total	$905.89	$196.83		

Balance Sheet
A Balance Sheet is another important report to include in your financial statements. It provides a snapshot of your business's financial situation at a defined point in time. Unlike a Profit and Loss Report which normally covers a month of transactions, a Balance Sheet reflects a specific time. This means that it can differ greatly from day to day based on your business transactions. Some writers create this report once a month to provide an update of their financial picture, others create a Balance Sheet once a year at the end of their accounting period (i.e.: December 31st). As we have learned, the Profit and Loss Report shows income and expenses in one financial document. A Balance Sheet shows the state of your business in more detail by looking at your business assets, liabilities, and equity. The Balance Sheet is divided into three distinct sections: assets, liabilities, and equity.

Assets

Assets are tangible and intangible items of value to your business. They are included on the Balance Sheet in descending order based on the level of liquidity. An asset's liquidity is the ease with which the asset can be converted into cash.

Current assets are shown first. The most liquid asset is cash. Your cash balance can also be called your petty cash. A checking or savings account would be listed first. This would be followed by the balance of Accounts Receivable (if your bookkeeping is utilizing the accrual method of accounting) and then fixed assets such as office furniture and equipment. If you had an inventory of your books and sold them to the public, you could include the value of your inventory as an asset as well. It may be helpful to refer back to your Inventory List in Chapter 3 when completing your Balance Sheet. You will find assets there which can be recorded on your personalized Balance Sheet.

Liabilities

Liabilities are funds that your business owes to another entity. This entity may be a person or business. These are also listed in descending order of liquidity. Furthermore, they are usually divided into current and long term liabilities. Current is generally considered due within a period of 12 months or less. Long term would be due in more than 12 months. Liabilities can include a business loan or taxes that you have collected which are due such as sales tax. This section can also be used to record your Accounts Payable if you are using the accrual method of accounting.

Equity

Equity is the amount of funds the owner has invested in the company less any owner draws (deductions). Current earnings would be listed here. Current earnings are your net profit or loss as reported on your Profit and Loss Report for the most recent period. As your company grows and you create subsequent Balance Sheets, an account called Retained Earnings can be added to this section. This is used to show your ongoing profit or loss from previous reports. If the Balance Sheet is completed correctly, the assets listed will match the total of liabilities plus equity. The physical structure of your Balance Sheet will include the company name on the top line and the date the Balance Sheet is being created on the next line. Beneath this, the traditional format for the report is to list the assets on the left column and then liabilities followed by equity on the right column.

Writer's Block

My gift is writing, not crunching numbers. Why do I have to track income and expenses?
—Lisa in New Hampshire

We all have to report our earnings to the IRS. No question about it. If we track our expenses we can reduce the income we pay tax on thus reducing our income tax liability. Therefore, tracking income and expenses will actually save us money!

There will be a total under each column and subtotals within. You can see how this works by viewing the example below for Write Now. You can also use the blank form in Chapter 10 to fill out a Balance Sheet for your business.

Write Now
Balance Sheet for November 30,

Current Assets		Current Liabilities	
Petty Cash	25.25	Start Up Loan Payable	500.00
Savings Account	2275.20		
Checking Account	324.90		
		Total Current Liabilities	500.00
		Long Term Liabilities	
Total Current Assets	2625.35		
Long Term Assets			
Computer	400.00	Total Long Term Liabilities	0.00
Office Desk	200.00	Total Liabilities	500.00
		Equity	
		Owner Equity	600.00
		Current Earnings	2125.35
		Retained Earnings	0.00
Total Long Term Assets	600.00	Total Equity	2725.35
Total Assets	3225.35	Total Liabilities & Equity	3225.35

Income Projections

Once you have been in business for six months, it is a good time to take a look at your income and expenses to determine if you have generated a profit or a loss. In accounting we call this a projection. We can look at your current financial statement and, after allowing for known variances, provide an estimate of future income.

This is useful for the growth of your business and for making estimated federal and state income tax payments. Armed with this information you can also adjust your tax payments to avoid penalties and interest charges for underpayment.

To complete a projection, you will look at your Profit and Loss Report for the six month period. List the total income and total expenses for this period on one financial report. Following the previous example, be sure to include both direct and indirect expenses.

When expenses are deducted from your income, you are left with your gross profit or loss recorded on the bottom line. This method of reporting does not allow for depreciation, but it does provide you with an estimate of your financial picture to date and enables you to project your total profit or loss for the year.

To arrive at your projected income for the year, you would double the net profit or net loss determined by this six month Profit and Loss Report.

Of course, we are assuming that the level of both income and expenses during the second six month period will remain consistent with the first six month period. It is wise to make adjustments if you know in advance that you will be accepting three new clients (increase in income) or that you were going to make a large purchase for your business such as a new computer (increase in expenses).

This projection is a valuable management tool which will enable you to make more informed business decisions. If your projection reveals a loss, you can examine your income and spending. Are you charging enough for your services? Are you spending too much on cases of paper?

On the other hand, if you are looking at a projected profit, you may want to consider the possibility of making quarterly estimated tax payments to avoid a big surprise when your income taxes are filed.

Business Plan

Every writing business should have a business plan. It can be very detailed, especially if you will be utilizing it to obtain a loan or grant, or it can be more of an informal summary of your business ideas.

To create a business plan, you need to thoroughly research your idea and understand what is required to succeed. When starting a writing business, a business plan is important and will help guide you down the right path for profit. Even if you have been freelance writing for years, preparing a business plan is a good idea because it can help refine your business goals and maintain the success you have started to achieve.

The first step in writing the plan is to organize your ideas. You will need to consider who your business is targeting, know your competition and how you can stand apart from them, think through the risks involved, and have a clear understanding of how much money will be required. When you are ready, it is time to sit down and write your plan.

Tips for Success
"Never stop marketing! Every time you write a piece, you can find several markets for it. Just a little tweaking can make the information interesting to a different market."

Patrika Vaughn, known as the world's foremost Authors' Advocate
www.acappela.com

ⓌⓇⒾⓉⒺⓇⓈ ⒷⓁⓄⒸⓀ

Why do I need to bother spending all this time writing a business plan? I'm not applying for loans or grants. What's the point?
—Brendan in Washington

Business plans are required by most lenders you may approach for business loans, but they are useful for so many other purposes. I would say the primary reason for writing your business plan is to increase the likelihood of business success. Going through the steps involved in writing a business plan takes you from the inception of your idea through the reality of day-to-day operations and leads you to the results you would like to achieve. It's time consuming to create a business plan, but well worth the energy and time you invest.

The first part of a business plan is called the Executive Summary. This is your chance to capture the attention of the reader and make your business shine. Try to keep this to no more than two typed pages, but use the space wisely.

As you continue to write your business plan, you will need to cover several aspects of business management. It is customary for a business plan to be in a report format consisting of several pages, a Table of Contents, and a cover. Your cover should include the name of your business, the address and phone number, along with the date on which the plan was prepared.

You can have your plan bound by a printer or you can use a three-ring view binder. The final document should portray a professional image.

Your goal in creating a business plan is to construct the most comprehensive document possible in order to achieve your career goals, direct your energies, and build your business with a solid foundation. A sample table of contents is included here as a guide.

Write Now Business Plan

Table of Contents

A comprehensive business plan will take time to create, but will help ensure the success of your new business. Remember, business plans are a work in progress. Be sure to review and update it as your company grows.

Business management involves managing the finances as well as the goals of your writing business. Keeping track of the profits and losses for your business will help you be more organized when you file your taxes. Knowing and understanding these numbers is essential to the success and longevity of your writing business.

Chapter 9

Taxes & Audits

This is a good time to share a few thoughts about paying taxes as a small business owner. As the owner of a business, your method of compensation is based on the legal organization of your business. You have the option of being an employee of the business if you are operating as an S-Corporation, but not as a sole proprietor. As a sole proprietor, you are subject to self-employment taxes.

Self-Employment Taxes

Self-employment tax is your contribution to the Social Security system. Social Security tax is 12.4% and Medicare tax is 2.9% based on 2008 earnings. This tax is due when sole proprietors file an annual tax return and is calculated using Federal Schedule SE, *Self-Employment Tax*. Half of this tax can also be taken as a deduction on the first page of your 1040 tax return. This deduction will reduce your taxable income.

Estimated Taxes

When you are an employee, taxes are withheld from your paycheck and sent in to the Internal Revenue Service, state, city, and local tax departments. As a business owner, you may need to make estimated tax payments to cover your liability since the IRS is a pay as you go system. If you need to make estimated payments, they are due four times each year: January, April, June, and September.

The amount you pay is based on taxable income from your business, other sources of income, deductions, taxes, and credits you may qualify for during that tax year. The IRS Web site offers form 1040-ES, *Estimated Tax for Individuals*, to assist you in determining estimated taxes.

Once this form is complete, if you determine estimated taxes are warranted, you can print out a payment voucher and mail it in with your payment by the deadline each month. An address is provided on the form.

As a writer, your income can fluctuate so it is a good idea to complete this form a few times each year. If you owe any federal tax, chances are you will owe state tax as well. This is a separate tax which varies by state. Be sure to check with your state tax department for compliance.

Tips for Success
"Save a percentage from EVERY check you get. This is so important I can't stress it enough. Above and beyond the money you set aside for quarterly taxes, you should also be adding to a liquid savings account."

Jess Sand, Copywriter Principal, Roughstock Studios
www. roughstockstudios.com

Tax Troubles

If estimated payments are required, based on the result of the 1040-ES form, and are not paid, the IRS may charge you interest and penalties on what you should have paid. If you are not able to make the estimated payments, the IRS does have the law on its side and can seize property and wages to satisfy debt. If you find yourself in this situation it is important to retain the services of a tax preparer, accountant, or lawyer with experience in this area.

Be sure to stay in touch with the IRS and document everything that transpires. Keep copies of all correspondence they send to you and copies of your replies. When on the telephone with an IRS agent, note the date, time, agent's name, and badge number along with the points of your conversation.

There are forms you can file requesting extensions (Form 1127 and Form 4868), installment payments (Form 9465), and even an Offer in Compromise (Form 656). Remember, the key is to keep the lines of communication open.

Audits

Just the mere mention of an IRS audit can bring fear into the heart of most people. Although it can be unsettling, if you have maintained your records and have the proper documentation to substantiate your claims, the audit will be smooth.

How does the IRS decide who is audited? There are many ways they determine who to audit. A few methods are discussed here. When tax returns are processed by the IRS, they are given a numeric score. This number is based on how many deductions claimed that are above or below the accepted average. The higher your score, the more likely it is you will be selected for an audit.

The numerical scoring system is kept secret, but industry professionals can attest to some red flag areas that have generated audits in the past. These can include higher than normal auto expenses, high travel or entertainment expenses, and little or no profit from a business. Even though the IRS does not divulge their scoring techniques, they do make some data available. The following table contains information based on the 2004 tax year which is currently the most recent available.

This information compares Adjusted Gross Income brackets along the top of the table to commonly deducted expenses down the side. For example, a taxpayer earning $50K–$100K should have estimated medical expenses of $6,125.00. If you fit into this earning bracket and claimed $35,000.00 instead of the $6,125.00 norm, your tax return could be flagged.

Average Deductions by Adjusted-Gross-Income Level

Income Level	$30K–50K	$50K–100K	$100K–200K	$200K & up
Interest expense	$6,933	$8,310	$10,949	$19,721
State and local income taxes	3,592	5,808	10,548	38,143
Contributions	2,132	2,663	4,130	19,014
Medical	5,324	6,125	9,811	31,332

Source: IRS Statistics of Income Bulletin (April 2006).

The entity you select to operate your business under can also be a target for audits. Unfortunately, most writers are considered small business owners and file as sole proprietors, a Federal Schedule C. Statistically, the IRS has audited a much higher percent of sole proprietors than other corporate entities. For example, in tax year 2005, a Schedule C filer had a one in 33 chance of being audited. For S-Corporations, the chances of being audited decreased to one in 300. As a business owner, you need to be prepared, document all allowable expenses and report all income. As long as you are following the rules, there is no need to panic.

Types of Audits
There are four kinds of audits ranging from simple correspondence to detailed in-person exams.

1. The Correspondence Audit is when the IRS sends you a letter requesting further documentation of certain expenses to substantiate deductions on your tax return.

2. The Office Audit comes by mail, but requires an in-person examination. The letter will list specific information that is in question and require you to meet at an appointed time with documentation to prove your deductions. It is not required, but it is recommended you bring a representative such as a tax preparer or certified public accountant (CPA) with you to this sort of audit.

3. The Field Audit normally begins with a phone call from an agent of the IRS. An appointment will be set for the auditor to come to you, the taxpayer. If you are selected for this type of audit, it is imperative you have an experienced representative to guide you.

4. The Taxpayer Compliance Measurement Program (TCMP) also called National Research Program audit, is a comprehensive audit in which every part of your tax return needs to be substantiated by documentation. Each line item will be examined and, again, representation is a must.

Tips for Surviving an Audit
There are some basic tips that can help you survive an audit.
- Stay calm.
- Present organized information.
- Provide supporting documents such as the logs kept in this book, receipts, and cancelled checks.
- Never give the IRS agent more or less information than is requested.
- Always answer honestly, but briefly.
- Never give original documents to the IRS—exchange copies only and keep originals for your records.

Remember, whether you prepared your tax return or hired another to complete it, you are ultimately responsible for the information it contains. Be sure to review your tax return and ask questions if something is not clear. If you are selected to be audited, you will need to prove your expenses and income.

Are You Ready to Meet the Tax Preparer?
Before you set up that appointment, you need to be sure that you have accounted for all of your income and allowable expenses. You also need to have the documentation to prove your claims are valid. Since you have been using the system outlined in this book, gathering the required information should be easy. All forms and receipts are in one, convenient, completely organized system.

Tips for Success
"If you loathe the financial side of the writing life, then beg or borrow the money to hire a pro. Since you are self-employed, doing it badly is the worst choice of all."

Nina B.
Independent Journalist
www.
bouncingbabyboomers.
com

Look at your Monthly Direct Expense Forms. Record the totals from these monthly logs onto your Annual Direct Expense Form. Transfer totals from your Monthly Indirect Expense Forms to your Annual Indirect Expense Form.

Transfer totals from your Monthly Income Forms to your Annual Income Form. If you have received any 1099-MISC tax forms from people or businesses you worked with during the year, be sure to bring these forms with you.

Review your Inventory List to be sure everything is accounted for. On the Automobile Registration Form, write down your ending odometer reading as of December 31st and be certain all of your mileage from the Monthly Direct Expense Forms have been recorded here. You will find blank forms for all of this in Chapter 10.

Give your Entertainment and Travel Logs a thorough review and verify all pertinent receipts have been attached to each log. This is an area where the IRS frequently explores in great depth. Those receipts and your documentation will help support your deduction.

Present this information along with your Balance Sheet dated 12/31 and your Profit and Loss Report covering the entire year you have been operating your business. With this information, your tax preparer will be able to complete your business tax return accurately and efficiently which should result in savings for you.

Not only should your income tax liability be lower since you have documented every possible deduction afforded to you as a writer, but you have also saved your preparer hours of sorting through a shoe box filled with confusing receipts which should reduce the fee you pay the preparer to file your taxes. Here is a checklist of what you should bring with you when you meet your preparer.

Tax Preparation Check List

Monthly Direct Expense Forms	Annual Direct Expense Form
Monthly Indirect Expense Forms	Annual Indirect Expense Form
Monthly Income Forms	Annual Income Form & 1099-MISC
Inventory List	Automobile Registration Form
Entertainment Logs	Travel Logs
Year End Balance Sheet	Year End Profit and Loss Report

Conclusion

My purpose for writing this book has been to assist writers with understanding and tracking their business income and expenses. Be sure to save every receipt, record every mile driven for business, and maintain your recordkeeping system on a regular basis.

By using the system described in this book, you will be able to record and prove all income and every expense related to the operation of your writing business. You will have all of the data organized with receipts attached and be completely prepared for annual tax filing. One of the most valuable business attributes is organization and you can attain it with regular use of this recordkeeping system. Good luck with your writing business!

Chapter 10

Blank Forms

Monthly Income Form
For the Month of _____

Date	Customer	Payment	Check	Balance
	Total			

Annual Income Form
For the Year of: _____

Month	Income
January	
February	
March	
April	
May	
June	
July	
August	
September	
October	
November	
December	
Total	

Notes for Next Year

Monthly Direct Expense Form
For the Month of _____

Date	Check	Payee	Description	Amount
		Total		

Annual Direct Expense Form
For the Year of: _____

January

Expense Category:						Total
Amount:						

Expense Category:						Total
Amount:						

February

Expense Category:						Total
Amount:						

Expense Category:						Total
Amount:						

March

Expense Category:						Total
Amount:						

Expense Category:						Total
Amount:						

April

Expense Category:						Total
Amount:						

Expense Category:						Total
Amount:						

May

Expense Category:						Total
Amount:						

Expense Category:						Total
Amount:						

June

Expense Category:						Total
Amount:						

Expense Category:						Total
Amount:						

July

Expense Category:						Total
Amount:						

Expense Category:						Total
Amount:						

August

Expense Category:						Total
Amount:						

Expense Category:						Total
Amount:						

September

Expense Category:						Total
Amount:						

Expense Category:						Total
Amount:						

October

Expense Category:						Total
Amount:						

Expense Category:						Total
Amount:						

November

Expense Category:						Total
Amount:						

Expense Category:						Total
Amount:						

December

Expense Category:						Total
Amount:						

Expense Category:						Total
Amount:						

Inventory List

Description	Purchase Date	Business Use	Cost	Value	Business Use Percentage

Indirect Monthly Expense Form
For the Month of _____

Category	Monthly Expense
Electric	
Garbage/Recycling	
Home Heating	
Home Insurance	
Indirect Repairs	
Mortgage Interest/Rent	
Property Tax	
Water/Sewer	
Other:	
Total	

Total Square Feet In Home			Total Number of Rooms In Home	
OR				
Total Square Feet In Home Office			Total Number of Rooms In Home Office	

Percent of Home Used by Home Office: _____

Indirect Annual Expense Form
For the Year of _____

Month	Electric	Garbage/ Recycling	Heating	Insurance	Repairs	Mortgage Interest or Rent	Prop Tax	Water/ Sewer	Other
Jan									
Feb									
Mar									
Apr									
May									
June									
July									
Aug									
Sept									
Oct									
Nov									
Dec									
Total									

Method 1
IRS Adjusted Mileage Allowance Form
Business Use Only
For the Period of: _____

Date	Beginning Odometer	Ending Odometer	Total	From	To	Purpose

Total Business Miles This Period	
Previous Business Miles	
Year to Date Business Miles	

Method 2
Actual Expense Form
Note if Use is Business (B) or Personal (P)
For the Period of: _____

Date	Beginning Odometer	Ending Odometer	Total	From	To	Purpose and <u>B</u> or <u>P</u>

	Business	Personal
Total Miles		
Previous Miles		
Year to Date Miles		

Automobile Registration Form	
Make	
Model	
Year of Manufacture	
Year Placed in Business Use	
Beginning Miles—January 1,	
Business Miles	
Personal Miles	
Ending Miles—December 31,	

Annual Summary

Month	Personal Miles	Business Miles	Automobile Expenses
January			
February			
March			
April			
May			
June			
July			
August			
September			
October			
November			
December			
Total			

Entertainment Log
For the Period of: _____

Date	Location	Purpose	Amount

Travel Log
For the Period of: _____

Date	Location	Purpose	Amount

Profit and Loss Statement
For the Period of: _____

Income:	Amount	Total
Total Writing Income		
Other Income:	Amount	Total
Total Other Income		
Total Income		
Expenses: Direct	Amount	Total
Total Direct Expenses		
Expenses: Indirect	Amount	Total
Total Indirect Expenses		
Total Expenses		
Profit or Loss		

Accounts Receivable Summary
For the Period of: _____

Source	Current	Past Due ____ Days	Past Due ____ Days	Past Due ____ Days
Total				

Accounts Payable Summary
For the Period of: _____

Payee	Current	Past Due _____ Days	Past Due _____ Days	Past Due _____ Days
Total				

Balance Sheet
Name of Business: _____
Date of Report: _____

Assets		Liabilities	
Current Assets		Current Liabilities	
Petty Cash		Accounts Payable	
Savings Account		Business Credit Card	
Checking Account			
Accounts Receivable			
		Total Current Liabilities	
		Long Term Liabilities	
Total Current Assets			
Long Term Assets			
Office Furniture		Total Long Term Liabilities	
Office Equipment		Total Liabilities	
Book Inventory		Equity	
Copyrights		Owner Equity	
		Current Earnings	
		Retained Earnings	
Total Long Term Assets		Total Equity	
Total Assets		Total Liabilities & Owner Equity	

Resources for Your Writing Business

American Screenwriters Association
www.asascreenwriters.com

American Society of Journalists and Authors
www.asja.org

The Authors Guild
www.authorsguild.org

Internal Revenue Service
www.IRS.gov

The International Women's Writing Guild
www.iwwg.com

National Association of Science Writers
www.nasw.org

National Writers Union
www.nwu.org

Romance Writers of America
www.rwanational.org

Small Business Administration
www.sbaonline.sba.gov

Small Publishers, Artists, and Writers Network
www.spawn.org

Social Security Administration
www.ssa.gov

United States Copyright Office
www.copyright.gov

Writer's Digest
www.writersdigest.com

Writers Guild of America
www.wga.org

Writer's Resource Center
www.poewar.com

Glossary

accounts payable Money that the business owes to others for services or products.

accounts receivable Money that is owed to the business from others for services or products.

accrual method of accounting In this method of bookkeeping, income is reported when it has been earned and expenses when they have been incurred.

advance A payment made before it is due and sometimes before the project has started.

aging accounts A periodic report showing all outstanding balances broken down by customer and by month or week due.

amortization A method of debt reduction in which a portion of the interest and principal is paid periodically. Also refers to gradually reducing the cost or value of an asset with periodic reductions over the projected life of the asset.

asset An item of value owned.

audit A formal examination of an individual's or company's tax return and supporting documentation used to verify that the information provided is accurate.

backup withholding Federal, State, and Local government agencies can place liens on any money due to taxpayers. These liens can be referred to as back up withholding.

balance sheet An important report to include in your financial statements that provides a snapshot of the financial situation of the assets, liabilities, and equity of your business at a defined point in time.

barter This is an exchange of property or services without involving the exchange of money.

cash method of accounting When using this method of bookkeeping, the business owner only reports income when it is actually received and expenses when they are actually paid.

consignment sale When an item is given or transferred to another entity to be sold and no payment is expected until the item is actually sold.

cost basis The amount exchanged to acquire a property. It can be adjusted to reflect when the property increases in value and when the property loses value.

depreciation To deduct from taxable income a portion of the original cost of a business asset over a specific number of years as the value of the asset decreases. To be depreciable, the asset must have a useful life that extends over one year.

direct business expense An expenditure that is directly related to the cost of operating your business.

equity This is the amount of funds the owner has invested in the company less any owner draws (deductions). It is also the monetary value of a property or interest in a property in excess of liens or claims against it.

exempt To be determined as free or released from a liability others are subject to.

expense An item of business outlay used to decrease revenue.

fair market value An amount that the buyer and seller are willing to agree to of their own free will.

gain An increase in value of an asset or property; selling an asset or property for more than it was originally acquired for.

gross The overall total amount before anything is deducted.

hybrid method of accounting This is a combination of the cash and accrual accounting methods.

incidentals These are miscellaneous expenses such as tips to a baggage carrier for a qualified business trip or gratuity paid to a waiter for a qualified business meal.

independent contractor A person or business that provides products or services to another according to the agreed upon terms. This is not to be confused with an employee, which works for the company.

indirect business expense An expenditure that is indirectly related to the cost of operating your business.

intangible property Not a physical item that can be touched; examples would be goodwill, copyright, trademark.

investment The outlay of money usually for income or potential profit.

liability Funds or debt that you or your business owe to another entity.

limited liability Where a business is held liable for its loans and debts and the business owner is not. Personal assets of the owner are protected and recognized as separate from the business assets.

liquidity Capable of being converted to cash.

loss A reduction in value of an asset or property; selling an asset or property for less than it was originally acquired for; when a business' expenses exceeded its income.

necessary expense An expenditure that is appropriate for the business you are operating.

net profit The result of a company's total expenses subtracted from the total income; where there is a surplus of income.

networking An exchange of information or services between individuals or groups, primarily to increase business relationships.

ordinary expense A common and accepted expense in your industry and profession.

partnership A form of legal business organization owned and managed by two or more entities, or partners, who join to carry on a trade or business. Each partner contributes to and shares in the profits and losses of the business. Partners pay any tax liability due, not the partnership.

petty cash This is your on hand cash available to be used for business purchases or expenditures.

profit and loss statement A report that shows you how much money you earned and how much money you spent. If the result is a positive number, the report is considered to show a profit. If the result is a negative number, it is considered to show a loss.

projection An estimate of future possibilities for income and expenses based on current trends.

recapture The act of being retaken. Can refer to taxes deducted on an income tax return which are later deemed invalid. The taxes deducted are recaptured in another tax year.

reimbursement To pay someone back or to make a payment equivalent to.

remit To send something such as money to another person or entity especially in response to a demand for payment.

S-Corporation A form of legal organization offering the avoidance of double taxation (once to the owners and again to the corporation) by electing to be treated as an S-Corporation. Owners, referred to as shareholders, pay tax—not the S-Corporation.

self-employment tax The taxes self-employed business owners have to pay towards Social Security and Medicare taxes.

sole proprietorship This is a non-incorporated form of legal organization for a business owned by one person.

straight-line method of depreciation A way to calculate the depreciation of an asset that suggests the asset will lose an equal amount of value for each year of its useful life.

subcontractor An individual or business hired to complete all or part of a project for another. This is not an employee of the entity who pays the subcontractor.

tangible property Something you can see and touch.

tax deduction An amount that may be subtracted from taxable income.

tax identification number An identification number used by Federal and State government agencies to identify a person or business. Individuals are issued Social Security numbers and businesses are issued Employer Identification numbers.

taxable income The amount of income that can be taxed by Federal, State, and Local agencies related to your business transactions.

unlimited liability An investment in which a person's personal and business assets are at risk of being lost. Owners can be held liable personally for the debts and liabilities incurred by the business.

unreimbursed expenses Payments made to another in the course of conducting business that are allowable income tax deductions which have not been paid by a third party.

About the Author

Brigitte A. Thompson is the founder and President of Datamaster Accounting Services, LLC in Vermont. She has been active in the field of accounting since 1986 and is a member of the American Institute of Professional Bookkeepers, the Vermont Tax Practitioners Associaton, and the Women Business Owners Network.

She is the author of several recordkeeping books for business owners, contributing author to two business books, and a freelance writer whose articles have appeared nationally in print and online publications.